OTHERWISE

OTHERWISE

Last and First Poems of
EUGENIO MONTALE

translated from the Italian by
Jonathan Galassi

Random House   New York

Thanks are due to the editors
of the following publications, in which some of these
translations originally appeared:
*Antaeus, The Nation, The New Criterion,
The New York Review of Books, The Paris Review,
Partisan Review, Stand,* and
The Threepenny Review.

Library of Congress Cataloging in Publication Data

Montale, Eugenio, 1896–1981
Otherwise : last and first poems of Eugenio Montale.

Translation of: Altri versi e poesie disperse.
Includes bibliographical references.
"Writings of Eugenio Montale": p.
I. Galassi, Jonathan.   II. Title.
PQ4829.O565A7813   1984   851'.912   84-42533
ISBN 0-394-52963-4

Manufactured in the United States of America
2   4   6   8   9   7   5   3
First American Edition

CONTENTS

UNCOLLECTED POEMS

EARLY POEMS, 1918–1928

LATER POEMS, 1962–1977

INTRODUCTION

Altri versi e poesie disperse, Montale's last book of poems, appeared in May 1981, a few months before his death.[1] The first section, "Altri versi" (or "Other Poems"), is an entire new collection, drawn from work written primarily in the late seventies and early eighties and composed in the diaristic manner that Montale adopted in his last decade, when he wrote enough new work to fill three books, nearly equaling in volume the production of his first forty years as a poet. The title I have given to the translation, *Otherwise*, is intended to suggest the speculative and often ambivalent nature of the meditations to which these poems give form.

The second section brings together poems from the full span of Montale's career that for various reasons were omitted from the poet's previous books. Most of the early work here predates or is contemporary with the poems included in his first book, *Ossi di seppia*, of 1925,[2] while the later group dates from the sixties and seventies. (A few of these last poems that depend on untranslatable wordplay or seem of minor interest have been omitted from the translation.)

This book, then, is representative of many Montales. The early poems give us what Lanfranco Caretti has called the Ur-Montale, the young apprentice trying on and discarding the styles and vocabulary of others as he discovers his own material and works toward the intense compression that was to become a hallmark of his greatest poetry. The notes at the back of the book discuss some of the major influences on these experiments; in many of them, however, classic Montalian themes—the portrayal of landscape to convey an interior state of being; an anxiety that is as much social as it is personal; woman

---

1. Most of the contents of this volume had already been published in the annotated edition of Montale's collected work, *L'opera in versi*, published by Gianfranco Contini and Rosanna Bettarini in 1980.
2. A few very early poems, from Montale's late teens, can be found in his *Quaderno genovese*, ed. Laura Barile (Milano: Mondadori, 1983).

as companion and muse, the embodiment of wholeness and salvation —can already be recognized.

Still, the dominant voice in *Altri versi* is the late Montale, the dry, wry, witty, often acerbic epigrammatist who, when he returned to poetry after a period of not writing in the fifties, abjured the highly composed if astringent lyricism of his first three books in favor of a terse, seemingly prosaic "critical" idiom. This new Montale, the poet of the *retrobottega*, or back of the shop, as he put it, emerged fully formed when he was in his seventies, with the publication of *Satura* (1971), the volume in which Montale collected the poems he had written since his third and arguably greatest book, *La bufera e altro* of 1956. In the poems of *Satura*, Maria Corti has written, "the dominant theme is the poet's tête-à-tête with this indecipherable world and some of the ideas pertaining to it: God, time, history, poetry, the *polis* . . . A coming to terms with great subjects, the attaining of a tone of universal meditation"[3] reminiscent of some of Montale's brief essays on social and cultural themes for Italy's leading newspaper, the *Corriere della Sera* of Milan. These same concerns dominate Montale's poetry from here on out, in the *Diario del '71 e del '72* (1973), the *Quaderno di quattro anni* (1977), and in *Altri versi*. Over time, the poems become increasingly more informal and less composed, more and more like extracts from an ongoing monologue. Not that Montale's late work is lacking in art; but the art becomes increasingly declarative and minimalist, more and more free of artifice. As with many creators in old age, the mere statement of a theme seems to suffice; its elaboration becomes superfluous.

Montale himself discussed the origins of his famous shift in style in a 1971 interview:

> Several years passed between my first three books and this fourth one, years spent in a formal profession which I did not have before—that of journalism, naturally—and in these intervening years I thought I would no longer write poems. Then, when I began to write a few epigrams, which were published at the bottom of short articles in the paper, the poetry spurted forth again and also took on a different, shall we say musical, dimension: the dimension of a poetry that tends toward prose and at the same time refutes it. And, from the phonic point of view, so to speak, I won't say this was an experiment, because there was no intentional experimentation, only a result. My former voice—poetry can

3. Maria Corti, " 'Satura' e il genere 'diario poetico' "; *Strumenti critici* (n. 15-giugno 1971), quoted in *Per conoscere Montale*, ed. Marco Forti (Milano: Mondadori, 1976), pp. 284–85.

always be compared to a voice—was, although no one ever said so, a voice that was still a bit "orotund" so to speak; actually, they said it was very prosaic even, but it isn't true; reread now I believe my work doesn't appear so. The new voice, however, is much enriched by harmonics and distributes them within the body of the composition. This was done largely unconsciously; then, when I had some examples of myself, shall we say, it may be that I followed the lessons I taught myself. But at the beginning, no, it was truly something spontaneous. . . .

[The use of contemporary terms in some of the poems] was necessary, given their episodic nature, rich in details, digressions, secondary themes, which then try to come together. Let's say there was a necessity for realism, although this word is a bit suspect today. Summing up my entire life in microscopic mini-episodes that were realistic, too, so to speak, it was quite necessary to have a language that distanced itself from the traditional.[4]

The realism to which Montale alludes here is an important notion to consider in reading his late poetry. It seems to involve a clear-sighted reading of contemporary experience that is always skeptical, and conscious of the distorting effects of received ideas. Implied is a disillusionment with politics and indeed with all forms of social organization, a hostility to the illusions of ideology. In a recent memoir the critic Ettore Bonora points out the congruity of Montale's attitude with the critical realism of modern epistemology, quoting an article by an Italian scientist about Montale's relationship to this strain of contemporary philosophic thought: "*Realism* [in this context] means the independence of reality in itself from our categories of thinking; *critical* signifies that this independent reality must first be edited (in the journalistic sense of the term) and organized by the mind in order to become an object of consciousness."[5]

It is this interplay between reality and "our categories of thinking" ("God, time, history, poetry, the polis"), through which we must perceive reality, that has been the major preoccupation of Montale's poetry since *Satura*. What Carlo Bo wrote about that book is equally true of the work that followed it: "The poems betray the same contradiction that characterizes Montale the man—the contradiction between a lucid and ruthless cruelty and a very pure feeling of love. *Satura* thus

4. Interview with Maria Corti in *L'approdo letterario* (n. 53—anno XVII—marzo 1971), quoted in Forti, pp. 85– 86.
5. Massimo Piattelli Palmarini, "Come un scienziato legge Montale," (*Corriere della Sera*, 4 nov. 1976), quoted in Ettore Bonora, *Conversando con Montale* (Milano: Rizzoli, 1983), pp. 79–80. According to Bonora, Montale considered this article one of the best about his work.

brings out the neat distinction between essence and representation, knowledge and realization, memory and miracle."[6] In poem after poem, our ways of organizing experience are submitted to relentless, often blistering, scrutiny. The frequent references to "the malicious invention of time," to life as a "performance," a "cabaret," and to the instability of the contemporary individual's sense of identity are only a few examples of Montale's radical questioning of the world-as-given. Yet we can see this same skepticism in embryonic form in the uncollected poems from the twenties, and can sense in them its roots in a frustrated idealism. The "tired day/that ends without apotheosis" at the end of the "Levantine Letter" of 1923 is not only a complaint against the etiolated nature of modern life; it also evokes a sense of impending threat, and reveals Montale's dependence—and that of his age—on a Christian teleology, an informing idea which no longer informs. We hear an echo of the same in the French fragment "You say our destinies of yesteryear have been recast," a first draft of the famous "Carnevale di Gerti" from Montale's second book, Le occasioni; and in "In the Void," the uncollected poem closest in method and language to the later work, where the poet and his companion wake to find themselves "prisoners from now on/of the vein that waits in the crystal for its hour."

But where the younger Montale evoked the saving experience found in flashes of illumination and brief instants of union with another, the later poetry is preoccupied with failures of communication, unrealized epiphanies, and the tragic inadequacy of all thought to embody contemporary truth. The so-called pessimism of much of Montale's work is related to this sense of disappointed expectation. Yet he himself has remarked that he does not know whether he is a pessimist or an optimist, that in fact these categories mean little for him.[7] Admitting that we do not know "what's beyond the blue" allows for the possibility that something outside the world of appearances may exist. An agnostic Christianity has always been at the root of Montale's skepticism and now that "the sun is really setting"—for himself and, he implies, for civilization as a whole—the poet returns again and again with poignant frequency (though often invoking his deeply ironic sense of humor) to the unresolved question of an afterlife.

This obsessive concern with the future is balanced by the digging-around in memory that dominates the second half of Altri versi. There

6. "Satura," in Agenda Vol. 9, No. 4–Vol. 10, No. 1 (Autumn–Winter 1971–72), p. 137.
7. See Bonora, pp. 124–25.

are poems about the author's youth in Genoa and the Cinque Terre, the famous landscapes from the poems of *Ossi di seppia* and *Le occasioni*; elegies for fellow writers and other artists; and poems re-evoking the women who are the protagonists of some of Montale's greatest work: the Clizia of the "Mottetti"; his wife, Drusilla Tanzi, known as La Mosca, to whom the "Xenia" are dedicated; and others. In these last poems, however, Montale's women appear less mythic and remote, less figural. Here they are actual individuals sketched with a few strokes, pieces of the past recalled by a yellowing photograph, rather than the alluring, evanescent actors they were in the symbolic dramas of the earlier poetry.

Yet they are no less affecting for that; indeed, when we consider their previous, always metaphysically weighted life in Montale's work, these characters come to life with a powerful terrestrialness, an almost ghostly realism, through the agonizing and tender contemplation of old age. As with much else in this book of relentless memory and meditation, these familiar presences, reexamined and renewed, provide us with new avenues of approach, new ways of thinking about this poet's seemingly inexhaustible major work. No one should mistake these last words for Montale at his greatest. They are too shorthand and fragmentary, and perhaps too resigned for that. Yet the manner and the matter remain unmistakable, giving us moment after moment of sudden brilliance and unforgettable beauty as the poet retraces his concerns, beliefs, doubts, and fears in a hand that is all the more haunting and insistent for its lightness of touch.

J. G.

OTHERWISE

POEMS
1972-1980

Altri versi

... cupole di fogliame da cui sprizza
una polifonia di limoni e di arance
e il velo evanescente di una spuma,
di una cipria di mare che nessun piede
d'uomo ha toccato o sembra, ma purtroppo
il treno accelera . . .

Notiziario ore 9 a.m.

Quel bischero del merlo è arrivato tardi.
I piccioni hanno già mangiato tutto.

L'inverno si prolunga, il sole adopera
il contagocce. Non è strano che noi
padroni e forse inventori dell'universo
per comprenderne un'acca dobbiamo affidarci
ai ciarlatani e aruspici che funghiscono ovunque?
Pare evidente che i Numi
comincino a essere stanchi dei presunti
loro figli o pupilli.
Anche più chiaro che Dei o semidei
si siano a loro volta licenziati
dai loro padroni, se mai n'ebbero.
Ma . . .

I

near Tellaro

. . . domes of foliage from which
a polyphony of oranges and lemons
glints with the evanescent veil of a mist,
a sea-foam no foot of man
has touched or so it seems, but unfortunately
the train picks up speed . . .

9 o'clock news

That fool of a blackbird came too late.
The pigeons have already eaten everything.

Winter lingers on. The sun is doled out
with a dropper. Isn't it strange that we,
lords and perhaps inventors of the universe,
to understand a piece of it, must trust
the charlatans and soothsayers mushrooming everywhere?
It seems obvious the Gods
are beginning to tire of their presumptive
children or wards.
Even clearer that, Gods or demigods,
they in turn have quit
their employers, if they ever had any.
But . . .

3

LE PULCI

Non hai mai avuto una pulce
che mescolando il suo sangue
col tuo
abbia composto un frappé
che si assicuri l'immortalità?
Così avvenne nell'aureo Seicento.
Ma oggi nell'età del tempo pieno
si è immortali per meno
anche se il tempo si raccorcia e i secoli
non sono che piume al vento.

PROSA PER A. M.

Forse si fu chiamati per lo spettacolo
ma l'attesa fu lunga e a cose fatte
rincasando nel gelo e rimbucandoci
là dove uscimmo per il nostro turno
si è incerti se tra il tutto e il nulla pesi
onesta e necessaria la bilancia.

Retrocedendo ed avanzando siamo
al tempo in cui la dolce Anne More
non resse all'undicesima gravidanza.
In tali casi sono male spesi
i curricula pronti per siffatte emergenze.
Resta il mistero perché tanto sangue
e inchiostro non poterono alla fine
rendere degustabile il cacciucco.
Fors'è per fare nascere la Poesia
e l'Averno con lei?
Tra l'orrore e il ridicolo il passo è un nulla.

THE FLEAS

Haven't you ever had a flea
that mixed its blood
with yours
concocting a frappé
that guaranteed us immortality?
It happened in the golden Sixteen Hundreds.
But today in the age of full time
it takes less to make us immortal
even if time is shrinking and the centuries
are only feathers in the breeze.

PROSE FOR A. M.

Maybe we were called for the performance
but the wait was long and in the end
going home in the cold back to the holes
we'd come out of for our turn
we're not sure that the scales between all and nothing
hang just and necessary.

Regressing and progressing, we
are in the time in which the sweet Anne More
didn't survive her eleventh pregnancy.
In such cases the commonplaces
prepared for like emergencies are wasted.
The mystery remains why so much blood
and ink could never make the chowder
palatable in the end.
Maybe to give birth to Poetry
and Hell as well?
The step between the horrific and the ridiculous is nothing.

MOTIVI

Forse non era inutile
tanta fatica
tanto dolore.

E forse pensa
così di noi e di sé
questo pseudo merlo orientale
che fischia nella sua gabbia
e imita la nostra voce.

C'è chi fischia di più
e c'è chi fischia di meno
ma anche questo è umano.

* * *

Costrette a una sola le sue punte
l'aragosta s'imbuca dove non si esce.
Per l'uomo non è questione di assottigliarsi.
O dentro o fuori non saprà mai che farsi.

* * *

Può darsi che sia ora di tirare
i remi in barca per il noioso evento.
Ma perché fu sprecato tanto tempo
quando era prevedibile il risultato?

* * *

Quando il fischio del pipistrello
sarà la tromba del Giudizio
chi ne darà notizia agli invischiati
nel Grande Affare?
Saremo a corto di comunicazioni,
in dubbio se malvivi vivi o morti.

THEMES

Maybe it wasn't useless
all this trouble
all this pain.

And maybe he thinks the same
of us and of himself
this oriental pseudo-blackbird
whistling in his cage
imitating our voice.

There are those who whistle more
and those who whistle less
but this too is human.

* * *

His two antennae narrowed down to one,
the lobster crawls into the hole you don't come out of.
For man it's not a question of thinning down.
He'll never know what to do, outside or in.

* * *

It may be time to pull
the oars into the boat for the dull event.
But why was so much time misspent
when the result was predictable?

* * *

When the bat's whistle
becomes the trumpet of Judgment
who'll tell the news to those ensnared
in the Great To Do?
We'll be short on information,
unsure if we're half-living, alive, or dead.

APPUNTI

I

A Caccia

C'è chi tira a pallini
e c'è chi spara a palla.
L'importante è far fuori
l'angelica farfalla.

II

Può Darsi

Può darsi che il visibile sia nato
da una bagarre di spiriti inferociti.
Ma tempo e spazio erano già creati?
Peccato, dice Crono al suo collega.
Si stava molto meglio disoccupati.

Amici, non credete agli anni-luce
al tempo e allo spazio curvo o piatto.
La verità è nelle nostre mani
ma è inafferrabile e sguiscia come un'anguilla.
Neppure i morti l'hanno mai compresa
per non ricadere tra i viventi, là
dove tutto è difficile, tutto è inutile.

Il big bang dovette produrre
un rombo spaventoso
e anche inaudito perchè non esistevano orecchie.
Queste giunsero solo
dopo molti milioni di millenni.

NOTES

I

Hunting

Some use grapeshot
some let bullets fly.
What matters is to do away
with the angelic butterfly.

II

It May Be

It may be the visible was born
from a melee of infuriated spirits.
But had time and space already been made?
Chronos says to his partner, Too bad.
We were much better off unemployed.

Friends, don't believe in light-years
in time or space whether curved or flat.
The truth is in our hands
but it's ungraspable and slithers away like an eel.
Not even the dead have ever understood it
so as to keep from falling back among the living
where all is difficult, all is useless.

The "big bang" must have produced
a terrifying boom
and unheard too because no ears existed.
These arrived only
after many millions of millennia.

Verità indiscutibile
che ci riempie di letizia
fatta eccezione per te mia capinera
che avevi stretto col tempo
un patto d'inimicizia
e l'hai rispettato perchè forse
ne valeva la pena – chi può dirlo?

A ZIG ZAG

Mi sono allungato sulla sabbia e rifletto.
Leggo la prosa di un Coboldo prete
d'assalto. Ma il pensiero va lontano.
Finito da due secoli il Concilio di Costanza
un pari d'Inghilterra poeta e puttaniere
ormai in punto di morte
negò recisamente la vita eterna e poi
per fare cosa grata al suo confessore
si convertì, ordinò alla moglie
di convertirsi, lei già sconvertita
passando ad altra confessione
e avrebbe convertito senza risparmio
presenti e assenti pur di farla finita.

Ora il sole sta veramente calando.
In fondo il buon Coboldo non ha tutti i torti.
Oggi non ci si ammazza più tra plausi e festeggiamenti.
Si sono scelti altri modi. Esistono 120
confessioni cristiane e pare che siano poche.

An undeniable fact
that strikes us as sublime
all except you, my blackcap,
who had made a pact
of enmity with time
and kept it, maybe because
it was worth it—who can say?

ZIG ZAG

I'm stretched out on the sand and thinking,
reading the prose of a certain Coboldo,
activist priest. But my thoughts wander.
Two hundred years after the Council of Constance
an English peer, poet and whoremonger
now on the point of death
firmly denied eternal life and then
to please his confessor, converted,
ordered his wife
(who'd already deconverted and gone on
to another faith) to reconvert
and would have endlessly converted
present and absent simply to end it all.

Now the sun is really setting.
In the end the good Coboldo isn't wholly wrong.
Today we no longer murder to plaudits and celebrations.
We've chosen other means. There are 120
Christian confessions; too few, it seems.

RIMUGINANDO

I

Probabilmente
sta calando la sera. Non per gli anni
che sono molti ma perchè lo spettacolo
annoiava gli attori più che il pubblico.
Non mi sono addentrato nella selva
né ho consultato San Bonaventura come C.
che Dio la protegga.
Non si tarda ad apprendere che gli anni
sono battibaleni e che il passato
è già il futuro. E il guaio è che l'incomprensibile
è la sola ragione che ci sostiene.
Se si fa chiaro che le Cause Prime
già contenevano in sé lo scoppio del ridicolo
si dovrà pure cercare altrove senza successo
perché l'avvenire è già passato da un pezzo.

II

Pare assodato che la vita sia nata
da una furente incompatibilità
di vapori e di gas e questo ci conforta
perché il cervello umano n'esce illeso.
L'infinito, il sublime e altri cacumi
se sono a nostro carico non ci caricano
di un ben fondato orgoglio. Non possumus.
Ma se n'esce incolpevoli. Le colpe
verranno dopo e sono incontestabili.
È il peccato d'orgoglio che dovrebbe
essere perdonato qualora un giudice
fosse a disposizione il che si nega
da più parti. E se poi così non fosse?

BROODING

I

Probably
evening is falling. Not because of the years
which are numerous but because the play
bored the actors more than the audience.
I haven't ventured into the forest
or consulted Saint Bonaventure like C.
may God preserve her.
It doesn't take long to learn that the years
are the twinkling of an eye and the past
is already the future. And the trouble is
the incomprehensible is the only reason that sustains us.
If it becomes clear the First Causes
already contained the explosion of the ridiculous
then we'll have to look elsewhere, though without success
since the future already passed some time ago.

II

It seems assured that life was born
from a raging incompatibility
of vapors and gases and this comforts us
because the human brain comes out unscathed.
The infinite, the sublime, and other heights,
even if they're our burden, don't burden us
with a well-founded pride. Non possumus,
but we come off blameless.
The blame comes later and it's incontestable.
It's the sin of pride that ought to be
pardoned, if a judge
were available, which is denied on several sides.
And what if it were otherwise?

OGGI

C'è qualcosa che squassa
che scoperchia e distrugge. Un punto perso da
Chi non vuole soccombere al Nemico.
Purtroppo noi poveri uomini siamo com'è
l'uccello in gabbia al volo degli storni.
Le nostre colpe saranno punite a colpi di scopa.
Non siamo che comparse, in gergo teatrale
utilités.
  A questo punto il poeta
lasciò la penna d'oca con la quale
componeva il poema Il ratto d'Europa
e si guardò allo specchio. Era lui,
era un altro, un demonio, un cerretano?
Forse l'Eco d'Europa, agenzia di encomiastici
soffietti, gli giocava un brutto tiro?
Poi si fece coraggio e riprese il Ratto
buttato nel cestino. D'altra parte
accanto a lui non c'erano animali
che fossero un doppione di se stesso.

NELL'ATTESA

Stiamo attendendo che si apra
la prima delle sette porte.
Era inutile mettersi decorazioni
dal collo fino al plastrone
perché l'attesa durerà un tempo
addirittura esponenziale.
Era inutile mettersi l'abito a doppia coda,
era inutile attendersi sinfonie di salmi
presentat arm di demoni forcuti
cerimonie o frustate, antipasti o cocktails di veleni.
Questa è la prima porta, non ha nessuna voglia

TODAY

There's something that shakes,
that flays and destroys. A point that's lost
on Those who won't succumb to the Enemy.
Sadly, we poor humans are like
the caged bird when the starlings fly.
Our sins will be punished with a good thrashing.
We're nothing but walk-ons, in theater slang,
utilités.
    At this point the poet
lay down the goose quill he was using
to write his poem, *The Rape* (or *The Rat*) *of Europa,*
and looked in the mirror. Was it he
or someone else, a demon, an impostor?
Perhaps the Echo of Europe, the positive
blurb service, was playing him a dirty trick?
Then he took heart and returned to the *Rat,*
which he'd tossed in the trash. Besides,
next to him there were no animals
who were doubles of himself.

WAITING

We're waiting for the first
of the seven doors to open.
There was no point pinning on ribbons
from neck to chest
because the wait will last a while
that's downright exponential.
There was no point putting on tails,
no point expecting symphonies of psalms
present-arms from horned devils
ceremonies or lashings, hors d'oeuvres or poison cocktails.
This door is the first, it has no wish to open

di aprirsi ma richiede un'etichetta.
Non era una follia parlare di porta stretta.
Le porte sono sprangate e a doppio lucchetto.
Forse qualcuno è riuscito a varcarle.
Ma era un uomo di *allora*, quando non esistevano
le parole che abbiamo.

L'ALLEVAMENTO

Siamo stati allevati come polli
nel Forward Institute
non quali anatre selvatiche o aquilotti
come chiedeva il nostro
immaginario destino.
E abbiamo annuito in coro intonando la marcia
En avant Fanfan-la-Tulipe!

Così
giusto è morire per una ingiusta causa.
Chi chiedesse una pausa
nella morìa sarebbe un traditore.
Ed è qui che il ridicolo si mescola
all'orrore.

IPOTESI II

Pare
non debba dirsi Italia ma
lo Sfascio.
È un fatto che si allunga, urge studiarlo
finché si esiste, dopo sarà tardi.

but it needs a name.
It wasn't folly to say that the gate was strait.
The doors are bolted with a double lock.
Maybe someone managed to get in.
But he was a man of *then*, when the words
we have today didn't exist.

OUR UPBRINGING

We were brought up like chickens
in the Forward Institute
not the wild ducks or eaglets
demanded by
our imaginary destiny.
And we nodded in unison, striking up the march,
En avant Fanfan-la-Tulipe!

So is it just
to die for an unjust cause.
Anyone who asked for a pause
in the plague would be a traitor.
And it's here the ridiculous
gets mixed up with the horror.

HYPOTHESIS II

It seems we shouldn't say Italy but
the Undoing.
It's a fact that reverberates, needs
to be studied while it lasts,
later will be too late.

Il tempo stesso ne sarebbe offeso;
mancando lo sfasciabile che cosa
potrebbe offrirci? È un tema che va messo
all'ordine del giorno.

Come si restringe l'orizzonte
a un certo punto.
Dove sono andati i vasti acquari
in cui si sguazzava
come il pesce nell'acqua senza il sospetto
della lenza e dell'amo.
                        La felicità
sarebbe assaporare l'inesistenza
pur essendo viventi neppure colti dal dubbio
di una fine possibile.
Dice un sapiente (non tutti sono d'accordo)
che la vita quaggiù fosse del tutto improbabile
col corollario (aggiungo) che non era
nient'affatto opportuna. Molti eventi
confortano la glossa. La sconfortano
piccoli *faits divers*; magari il volo
di una formica mai studiata o neppure vista
dagli entomologi.

La buccia della Terra è più sottile
di quella d'una mela se vogliamo supporre
che il mondo materiale non sia pura illusione.
Tuttavia in questo nulla, ammesso che sia tale,
siamo incastrati fino al collo. Dicono
i pessimisti che l'incastro include
tutto che abbiamo creato per surrogare i Dei.

Time itself would be offended;
without the undoable
what could it offer us? It's a subject that belongs
on the order of the day.

How the horizon
narrows at a certain point.
Where are the vast aquaria
we wallowed in
like fish in water, with no idea
of hook or line.
                    Happiness
would be savoring nonexistence
while living, unconcerned
with a possible end.
One wise man says (not everyone agrees)
that life down here was totally improbable
with the corollary (I add) that it wasn't
at all appropriate. Many events
support this interpretation. Little *faits divers*
contradict it; like the flight
of an ant that has never been studied or even seen
by the entomologists.

The crust of the Earth is thinner
than an apple's if we want to suppose
the material world isn't pure illusion.
Still in this nothing, given it is such,
we're stuck up to our necks.
The pessimists say the muck includes
everything we've made to replace the Gods.

Ma la sostituzione non fu feconda
affermano i fedeli del vecchio Dio.
Forse verrà Egli stesso dicono
a strapparci dal magma e a farsi vivo.
Siamo e viviamo dunque una doppia vita
sebbene l'egolatra ne vorrebbe una sola.

O madre Terra o cielo dei Celesti
questo è il guaio
che ci fa più infelici dell'uccello
nel paretaio.

L'ALLEGORIA

Il senso del costrutto non è chiaro
neppure per coloro che riguarda.
Noi siamo i comprimari, i souffleurs nelle buche
ma i fili del racconto sono in mano d'altri.
Si tratta chiaramente di un'allegoria
che dura da un'infinità di secoli supponendo
che il tempo esista oppure non sia parte
di una divina o no macchinazione.
Alcuni suggeriscono marchingegni
che facciano crollare il tutto su se stesso.
Ma tu non credi a questo: la gioia del farnetico
è affare d'altri.

VINCA IL PEGGIORE

disse Colui del quale non può dirsi il nome
ma poi fu preso dal dubbio
e il suo diktat lasciò aperto qualche buco.
Il vincitore il vinto

But the substitution wasn't fruitful
claim the faithful of the old God.
Maybe He himself will come, they say,
to pull us out of the mud and reveal himself.
Therefore we are and live a double life
even if the ego-worshipper would like only one.

O mother Earth, O heaven of the Blest
this is the trouble
that makes us more unhappy than the bird
caught in the net.

THE ALLEGORY

The sense of its construction isn't clear
even for those it concerns.
We're the supporting actors, the prompters in the pit,
but the threads of the tale are in the hands of others.
Clearly it's an allegory
which has lasted an infinity of centuries
supposing time exists or isn't part
of some machination, divine or otherwise.
Some suggest contraptions
that make everything collapse.
But you don't believe in this: the joy of the delirious
is other people's business.

MAY THE WORST MAN WIN

said He whose name cannot be said
but then he was seized by doubt
and his diktat left several loopholes.
Victor and vanquished,

il vivo il morto l'asino e il sapiente
stanno a contatto di gomito
anzi non stanno affatto
o sono in altro luogo
che la parola rifiuta.

Con quale voluttà
hanno smascherato il Nulla.
C'è stata un'eccezione però:
le loro cattedre.
Et tout le reste c'est du charabia
disse taluno; necessario anche questo
per ottenere il resto.

Una zuffa di galli inferociti
quella di casa nostra?
La differenza è
che colui che di tutto tiene i fili
non si accorge di niente
mentre l'applauso a questi spennamenti
è furente.

Non è crudele come il passero di Valéry
l'uccellino che viene a beccar poche briciole
quando s'alza o dirada qualche stecca
l'avvolgibile.

Anche per noi è questione di passaggi,
sia di sopra o di sotto. E le analogie
non si fermano qui. Fino a che punto
lo dicano i filosofi o i maestri
di bricolage fortunatamente
inascoltati è da vedersi.

living and dead, fool and wise man
are rubbing elbows
or they're not at all
or they're in another place
which the word denies.

With what joy
they unmasked the Void.
But there was one exception:
their professorships.
Et tout le reste c'est du charabia,
said one; which is necessary too
in order to get the rest.

A scuffle of furious cocks—
is it like that with us?
The difference is
that he who holds the strings to everything
doesn't realize a thing
while the applause at these defeatherings
is frantic.

He's not cruel like Valéry's sparrow,
the little bird who comes to peck a few crumbs
when the blind is raised or a few of its slats
are parted.

For us too it's a question of travel,
above or below. And the analogies
don't end here. How far
the luckily unheeded philosophers
or masters of bricolage say they go
remains to be seen.

L'avvenire è già passato da un pezzo.
Può darsi però che ammetta qualche replica
dato l'aumento delle prenotazioni.
Con un palmo di naso resteranno
gli abbonati alle prime; e col sospetto
che tutto involgarisce a tutto spiano.

Il grande scoppio iniziale
non dette origine a nulla di concreto.
Una spruzzaglia di pianeti e stelle,
qualche fiammifero acceso nell'eterno buio?
L'Artefice supremo era a corto di argomenti?
C'è chi lo pensa e non lo dice,
c'è chi pensa che il pensiero non esiste.
E che più? Forse l'Artefice pensa
che gli abbiamo giocato un brutto tiro.

È probabile che io possa dire io
con conoscenza di causa
sebbene non possa escludersi che un ciottolo,
una pigna cadutami sulla testa
o il topo che ha messo casa nel solaio
non abbiano ad abundantiam quel sentimento
che fu chiamato autocoscienza. È strano
però che l'uomo spenda miracoli d'intelligenza
per fare che sia del tutto inutile
l'individuo, una macchina che vuole
cancellando ogni traccia del suo autore.
Questo è il traguardo e che nessuno pensi
ai vecchi tempi (se mai fosse possibile!).

The future already happened a while ago.
But maybe it will allow repeat performances
given the increase in reservations.
At the openings the subscribers
will have long faces; and they'll suspect
that everything is becoming totally vulgar.

The big initial bang
gave rise to nothing concrete.
A spray of planets and stars,
some matches struck in the eternal dark?
Was the supreme Creator short on ideas?
Some think so but don't say it,
some think that thinking doesn't exist.
And what else? Maybe the Creator thinks
we've played him a dirty trick.

It's probable I can say I
with knowledge of cause
though it can't be excluded that a pebble
or a pinecone fallen on my head
or the mouse who has set up house in the attic
don't have ad abundantiam the feeling
that was called self-consciousness. Yet it's strange
that man should spend prodigies of intelligence
to make the individual totally useless,
a machine that wills,
erasing every trace of its creator.
This is the finish-line and let no one think
of the old days (even if it were possible!).

TEMPO E TEMPI II

Da quando il tempo-spazio non è più
due parole diverse per una sola entità
pare non abbia più senso la parola esistere.
C'era un *lui* con un peso, un suono, forse un'anima
e un destino eventuale, chissà come.
Ora bisogna sentirselo dire: tu sei tu
in qualche rara eccezione perché per distinguersi
occorre un altro, uno che con sottile artifizio
supponiamo diverso, altro da noi, uno scandalo!
Si presume che in fatto di velocità il corvo
(e anche d'intelligenza) possa dare dei punti
all'uomo. È un fatto discutibile. Ma
intanto lui vola con ali sue mentre tu
che della vita sapesti solo l'alba e tu
che lottando col buio avesti migliore destino
e il povero poeta (?) che ti disse
prenotami magari un posto di loggione
lassù se mi vedrai, abbiamo avuto il sospetto
di stringere qualcosa tra le dita.

Per quanto tempo? Ah sì c'è sempre la malefica
invenzione del tempo!

L'OBOE

Talvolta il Demiurgo, spalla di Dio e Viceré quaggiu,
rimugina su quali macchinazioni
gli attribuiscano i suoi nemici,
i fedeli al suo Dio perché quaggiù
non giungono gazzette e non si sa
che siano occhi e orecchie. Io sono al massimo
l'oboe che dà il *la* agli altri strumenti
ma quel che accade dopo può essere l'inferno.
Un giorno forse potrò vedere anch'io,

TIME AND TIMES II

Ever since time-and-space were not
two different words for one sole entity
it's seemed the word existence no longer has meaning.
There was a *he* with a weight, a sound, maybe a soul,
and, who knows how, a destiny ahead.
Now we need to be told: You're you
in some rare cases, for to distinguish ourselves
we need someone else, who with subtle artifice
we suppose to be different, other than us, a scandal!
It's presumed that in terms of velocity
(and intelligence) the crow scores over man.
This is debatable. Still,
he flies with wings of his own, while you
who knew only the dawn of life
and you who had better luck struggling with the dark
and the poor poet(?) who said to you,
Why not reserve me a seat up above
if you see me—we had the suspicion
we held something in our hands.

For how much time? Ah yes, always the malicious
invention of time!

THE OBOE

Sometimes the Demiurge, right hand of God and Viceroy down here,
broods on the machinations
ascribed to him by his enemies,
the faithful of his God, because down here
no newspapers arrive and no one knows
that there are eyes and ears. I am at most
the oboe that tunes the other instruments
but what happens later can be hell.
One day maybe I, though potent and blind today,

oggi possente e cieco, il mio padrone
e nemico ma penso che prima si dovrà inventare
una cosa da nulla, il Tempo, in cui
i miei supposti sudditi si credano sommersi.

Ma, riflette il Demiurgo, chissà fino a quando
darò la mano (o un filo) al mio tiranno? Lui stesso
non ha deciso ancora e l'oboe stonicchia.

LO SPETTACOLO

Il suggeritore giù nella sua nicchia
s'impappinò di certo in qualche battuta
e l'Autore era in viaggio e non si curava
dell'ultimo copione contestato
sin da allora e da chi? Resta un problema.
Se si trattò di un fiasco la questione
è ancora aperta e tale resterà.
Esiste certo chi ne sa più di noi
ma non parla; se aprisse bocca sapremmo
che tutte le battaglie sono eguali
per chi ha occhi chiusi e ovatta negli orecchi.

Colui che allestì alla meno peggio
il cabaret
tutto aveva previsto gloria e infamia
o cadde in una trappola
di cui fu prima vittima se stesso?
Che possa uscirne presto o tardi è dubbio.
È la domanda che dobbiamo porci
uomini e porci, con desideri opposti.

will be able to see my master and enemy
but before this I think a little nothing
will have to be invented: Time
in which my so-called subjects think they're immersed.

But, thinks the Demiurge, who knows how long
I'll lend a hand (or rope) to my tyrant?
He still hasn't decided himself and the oboe is going flat.

THE PERFORMANCE

The prompter down in his box
certainly missed a few bars
and the Author was traveling and didn't take charge
of the final score, which has been contested ever since
and by whom? It's still a problem.
Whether it was a fiasco
is and will remain an open question.
Surely there's someone who knows more about it than we do
but he isn't talking; if he opened his mouth we'd know
that all battles are the same
for those with their eyes shut and cotton in their ears.

Had he who staged the cabaret
as well as possible
foreseen everything, glory and infamy,
or did he fall into a trap
of which he was the first victim?
It's doubtful he can get out, early or late.
This is the question we have to ask ourselves,
men and pigs, with contrary desires.

Se l'universo nacque
da una zuffa di gas
zuffa non zuppa allora
com'è possibile, come ...
ma qui gli cadde di mano
quella penna di cigno
che seppure in ritardo
si addice ancora a un bardo.

Si può essere a destra
o a sinistra
o nel centro
o in tutt'e tre, che non guasta.
Ma tutto ciò presuppone
che l'Essere sia certo,
sia la buridda di cui ci nutriamo
quando sediamo a tavola.
Alas, poor Yorick, che teste di cavolo
noi siamo (e questa resta
la nostra sola certezza).

GIOVIANA

Si scrivono miliardi di poesie
sulla terra ma in Giove è ben diverso.
Neppure una se ne scrive. E certo
la scienza dei gioviani è altra cosa.
Che cosa sia non si sa. È assodato
che la parola uomo lassù desta
ilarità.

If the universe was born
from a stew of gases
a stew not a brew
then how is it possible, how . . .
but here the swan's quill
that still though it's late
belongs to the poet
fell from his hand.

You can be right
left
or center
or all three, no matter.
But all this presupposes
that Being is certain,
the bouillabaisse we feed on
when we sit at table.
Alas, poor Yorick, what dunderheads
we are (and this will be
our only certainty).

JOVIANA

Billions of poems are written on earth
but on Jupiter it's otherwise.
Not even one. And certainly
the Jovians' science is something else.
We don't know what it is. It's been confirmed
that up there the word man arouses
laughter.

Quando il mio nome apparve in quasi tutti i giornali
una gazetta francese avanzò l'ipotesi
che non fossi mai esistito.
Non mancarono rapide smentite.
Ma la falsa notizia era la più vera.
La mia esistenza fisica risultò un doppione,
un falso come quella planetaria
gode il discusso onore di questi anni.
Sarebbero dunque falsari gli astronomi o piuttosto
falsettanti? La musica vocale
abbisogna di questo o di simili trucchi.
Ma che dire del suono delle Sfere?
E che del falso, del vero o del pot pourri?
Non è compito nostro sbrogliare la matassa.
D'altronde anche filosofi e teologi
sono viventi in carne ed ossa. Ed ecco
il fabbisogno, il dovere di battere la grancassa.

IN ORIENTE

Forse divago dalla retta via.
Questa biforcazione tra Sunna e Scia
non distrugge il mio sonno ma fa di me l'alunno.
È come fare entrare lo spago in una cruna
d'ago.

ALL'ALBA

Lo scrittore suppone (e del poeta
non si parli nemmeno)
che morto lui le sue opere
lo rendano immortale.
L'ipotesi non è peregrina,

When my name appeared in almost all the papers
a French gazette advanced the hypothesis
that I'd never existed.
There were prompt denials,
but the false news was the truest.
My physical existence turned out to be a double,
a forgery like the planetary one
enjoys the public honor of these years.
Are the astronomers falsifiers then
or only falsettos? Vocal music
needs this or similar tricks.
But what about the music of the Spheres?
And what about the false, the true, the potpourri?
It's not our job to unravel the tangle.
Besides, even philosophers and theologians
are living flesh and blood. Whence come
the need and the duty to beat the big drum.

IN THE EAST

Perhaps I stray from the right way.
This parting of Sunnite and Shiite
doesn't keep me up but makes me use my head.
It's like putting thread
through a needle's eye.

AT DAWN

The writer supposes (let's not
even mention the poet)
that when he dies his works
will make him immortal.
The notion's not peculiar,

ve la do per quel che vale.
Nulla di simile penso nel beccafico
che consuma il suo breakfast giù nell'orto.
Egli è certo di vivere; il filosofo
che vive a pianterreno
ha invece più di un dubbio. Il mondo può
fare a meno di tutto, anche di sé.

MONOLOGO

Non mi affaccio più
dal parapetto
per vedere se arriva
la diligenza a cavalli
che porta gli scolari dai Barnabiti.
Poi lunghi tratti di vita
appaiono scancellati
mi sembra sciocco chi crede
che la vita non soffre interruzioni
non si tratta di morte e resurrezioni
ma di lunghe discese agl'Inferi dove ribolle
qualche cosa non giunta al punto di rottura
ma questo sarebbe la morte che detestiamo
così ci contentiamo di un ribollìo
che è come un tuono lontano,
qualcosa sta accadendo nell'Universo
una ricerca di se stesso
di un senso per poi ricominciare
e noi a rimorchio, cascami
che si buttano via
o cade ciascuno da sé.

I state it for what it's worth.
No such thought in the warbler
eating his breakfast down in the garden.
He's certain he's alive; but the philosopher
who lives on the ground floor
has more than one doubt. The world
can do without everything, even itself.

MONOLOGUE

I don't appear
at the parapet anymore
to see if the stage-
coach has arrived
bringing the students from the Barnabites.
Then long stretches of life
seem erased
I think only fools believe
life suffers no interruptions
I don't mean death and resurrections
but long descents into the Depths where something
that hasn't reached the breaking point is bubbling
but this would be the death that we detest
so we make do with a rumble
like distant thunder.
Something is happening in the Universe
a search for the self
for a reason to start over
and we are in tow, rags
that get tossed out
or fall on their own, one by one.

ALUNNA DELLE MUSE

Riempi il tuo bauletto
dei tuoi carmina sacra o profana
bimba mia
e gettalo in una corrente
che lo porti lontano e poi lo lasci
imprigionato e mezzo scoperchiato
tra il pietrisco. Può darsi che taluno
ne tragga in salva qualche foglio, forse
il peggiore e che importa? Il palato,
il gusto degli Dei sarà diverso
dal nostro e non è detto che sia il migliore.
Quello che importa è che dal bulicame
s'affacci qualche cosa che ci dica
non mi conosci, non ti conosco; eppure
abbiamo avuto in sorte la divina follìa
di essere qui e non là, vivi o sedicenti
tali, bambina mia. E ora parti
e non sia troppo chiuso il tuo bagaglio.

PUPIL OF THE MUSES

Fill up your satchel
with your sacred and profane
hymns, my girl
and toss it into a stream
that will carry it off and leave it
trapped and half-uncovered
in the rubble. Maybe someone
will pull a few sheets to safety,
maybe the worst and what does it matter?
The taste of the Gods will be different from ours
and nobody says that it's better.
What matters is that out of the seething mass
something appears that says to us,
You don't know me, I don't know you; and yet
it was our fate to have the divine madness
of being here and not there, living
or so we call it, my child. And now go
and may your bag not be too tightly shut.

ALL'AMICO PEA

Quando Leopoldo Fregoli udì il passo della morte
indossò la marsina, si mise un fiore all'occhiello
e ordinò al cameriere servite il pranzo.
Così mi disse Pea della fine di un uomo che molto ammirava.
Un'altra volta mi parlò di un inverno a Sarzana
e di tutto il ghiaccio di quell'esilio
con una stoica indifferenza che mascherava la pietà.
Pietà per tutto, per gli uomini, un po' meno per sé.
Lo conoscevo da trent'anni o più, come impresario
come scalpellatore di parole e di uomini.
Pare che oggi tutti lo abbiano dimenticato
e che la notizia in qualche modo sia giunta fino a lui,
senza turbarlo. Sta prendendo appunti
per dirci cosa è oltre le nubi,
oltre l'azzurro, oltre il ciarpame del mondo
in cui per buona grazia siamo stati buttati.
Poche note soltanto su un taccuino che nessun editore
potrà mai pubblicare; sarà letto forse
in un congresso di demoni e di dèi
del quale si ignora la data perché non è nel tempo.

II

TO MY FRIEND PEA

When Leopoldo Fregoli heard the footfall of death
he put on his tails, set a flower in his lapel
and ordered the waiter, Serve lunch.
Pea told me this about the end of a man he greatly admired.
Another time he talked about a winter in Sarzana
and all the ice of that exile
with a stoic indifference that masked his compassion.
Compassion for everything: for men, and a bit less for himself.
I knew him for thirty years or more as an impresario,
a shaper of words and men.
Today it seems everyone's forgotten him
and somehow the news has reached him too
without upsetting him. He's taking notes
to tell us what's beyond the clouds,
beyond the blue, beyond the junkheap of the world
we were tossed on by good grace.
Just a few lines in a notebook no publisher
will ever be able to print; perhaps it will be read
at a congress of demons and gods
the date of which is unknown since it isn't in time.

NIXON A ROMA

In numero restretto, setacciati
ma anche esposti a sassaiole e insulti
siamo invitati al banchetto
per l'Ospite gradito. Cravatta nera e niente
code e decorazioni. Non serve spazzolare
sciarpe e ciarpame. Saremo in pochi eletti
sotto i flash, menzionati dai giornali
del pomeriggio che nessuno legge.
Avremo i Corazzieri, un porporato,
le già Eccellenze e i massimi garanti
della Costituzione,
il consommè allo Sherry, il salmone, gli asparagi
da prender con le molle, il Roederer brut,
i discorsi, gli interpreti, l'orchestra
che suonerà la Rapsodia in blu
e per chiudere Jommelli e Boccherini.
Il cuoco è stato assunto per concorso
e per lui solo forse siamo all'Epifania
di un Nuovo Corso.
L'Ospite è giunto; alcuni
negano che sia stato sostituito.
Gli invitati non sembrano gli stessi.
Può darsi che il banchetto sia differito. Ma
ai toast sorgiamo in piedi coi bicchieri
e ci guardiamo in volto. Se i Briganti
di Offenbach non si sono seduti ai nostri posti
tutto sembra normale. Io dice il direttore
dei servizi speciali.

NIXON IN ROME

A limited number, sifted through
but exposed to stonings and insults too
we're invited to the banquet
for the honored Guest. Black tie
and no tails or decorations. No point brushing off
sashes or trash. We'll be a chosen few
under the flashbulbs, mentioned in the afternoon
papers that nobody reads.
We'll have the Honor Guard, an eminence,
their ex-Excellencies and the greatest
guarantors of the Constitution,
sherried consommé, salmon, asparagus
(handle with care), Roederer brut,
speeches, interpreters, the orchestra
will play Rhapsody in Blue
and at the end, Jommelli and Boccherini.
The cook was chosen by competition
and for him alone perhaps we're at the Epiphany
of a New Course of Action.
The Guest has arrived; some deny
he's a stand-in.
The invitees don't seem the same.
Maybe the banquet has been postponed.
But at the toasts we rise with glass in hand
and look each other in the face. If Offenbach's
Brigands aren't sitting in our places
everything seems normal. So says the editor
of Special Reports.

CÀFFARO

La vecchia strada in salita è via Càffaro.
In questa strada si stampava il Càffaro,
il giornale più ricco di necrologi economici.
Aperto in rare occasioni c'era un teatro già illustre
e anche qualche negozio di commestibili.
Mio padre era il solo lettore del Càffaro
quello dov'era dolce spengersi tra le braccia
d'infinite propaggini. Fornito di monocolo
col nastro il Direttore del giornale
e anche un suo alter ego con in più una mèche bianca
a cui doveva non poco lustro. Si diceva
che per arrotondare i suoi magri profitti
il dotto traduttore del Càffaro annalista
doveva essere lui ma poi l'impresa
passò ad altri e nessuno se ne dolse.
Col fiato grosso salivo a Circonvallazione.
Io con manuali scolastici, il Direttore scendeva
ma il suo occhio di vetro mai si fermò su me.
Di lui nulla si seppe. Più sconsigliato invece
il traduttore mancato portò sulla piccola scena
un suo drammone storico del quale in robone ducale
fu interprete l'Andò e andò malissimo
tanto che quando apparve la nota mèche al proscenio
un grido di bulicciu! divallò dalle alture
e fu l'unico omaggio che i suoi fedeli
se mai ne fu taluno vollero tributargli.

AL GIARDINO D'ITALIA

Larbaud

C'incontrammo al Giardino d'Italia
un caffè da gran tempo scomparso.
Si discuteva la parola romance
la più difficile a pronunziarsi, la sola
che distingue il gentleman dal buzzurro.

CÀFFARO

The old street that rises here is Via Càffaro.
On this street they printed *Il Càffaro*,
the paper that was richest in bankruptcies.
There was a once-famous theater, open on rare occasions,
and a few food shops too.
My father was the only reader of *Il Càffaro*,
the one where it was sweet to expire
in the arms of infinite offspring.
The Editor of the paper had a monocle with a ribbon
as did his alter ego, who also had a white streak
which earned him no little fame.
It was said that to round off his meager earnings
the learned translator of *Il Càffaro*
was forced to be its annalist as well,
but later the task passed to others and no one complained.
Panting, I climbed to the road that circles the city
with my schoolbooks. The Editor was coming down
but his glass eye never focused on me.
We knew nothing about him. But the neglected translator,
more ill-advised, produced
an historical drama of his own on the little stage.
Andò performed it in ducal robes and, oh, it was a flop,
so much so that when the famous streak appeared on stage
a shout of *bulicciu!* rang down from the balcony,
the only homage his faithful,
if he ever had them, were willing to pay him.

AT THE GIARDINO D'ITALIA

Larbaud

We met at the Giardino d'Italia
a café that has long since disappeared.
The word "romance" was discussed,
the most difficult word to pronounce,
the one that separates the "gentleman" from the boor.

Poi ordinò un ponce all'italiana
e la sua dizione era alquanto bigarrée
(ma è un eufemismo).
Vedevo in lui Lotario che battendo
di porta in porta ricerca la sua Mignon.
Per ritrovarla poi, mentre la mia
era perduta.

a Charles Singleton

Sono passati trent'anni, forse quaranta.
In un teatro-baracca si riesumava
una noiosa farsa dell'aureo Cinquecento.
Ne comprendevo assai poco ma tutto il resto
era per me decifrato da un provvido amico straniero
che poi scomparve. Lo avevo già visto al Caffè
degli scacchisti. Allora non sapevo
che non esistono rebus per il Patròlogo
ma un nome solo sfaccettato anche se unico.
C'è chi vorrebbe sopprimere anche quello.
Forse doveva essere l'opinione
del misterioso personaggio che ora si rifà vivo
perchè ricorda la sera del baraccone
ed il soccorso datomi. Del suo commercio coi Padri
non fece cenno. Sarebbe stato ridicolo.

LE PIANTE GRASSE

Un mio lontano parente era collezionista
di piante grasse. Venivano da ogni parte
per vederle. Venne anche il celebrato (?)
de Lollis delibatore di poesia prosastica.
Si erano conosciuti al Monterosa
ristorante per celibi ora scomparso.

Then he ordered an Italian punch
and his diction was somewhat bigarrée
(a euphemism).
In him I saw Lothario, knocking
on door after door in search of his Mignon.
And finding her, while my own
was lost.

to Charles Singleton

This was thirty, maybe forty, years ago.
In an outdoor theater they were exhuming
a boring farce from the golden Sixteenth Century.
I understood very little but all the rest
was deciphered for me by a provident foreign friend
who later disappeared. I'd already seen him
at the chess players' café. Then I didn't know
that there are no riddles for the Patrologist
but one name only, faceted if unique.
There are those who want to suppress even that.
Perhaps this was the opinion
of the mysterious character who shows up now
because he remembers that evening in the tent
and the help he gave me. Of his commerce with the Fathers
he gave no sign. It would have been ridiculous.

SUCCULENTS

A distant relative was a collector
of succulents. People came from everywhere
to see them. Even the famous (?)
de Lollis, connoisseur of prose-poetry.
They had met at the Monterosa,
a restaurant for bachelors that's disappeared.

Oggi non esistono più
le serre le piante grasse e i visitatori
e nemmeno il giardino dove si vedevano
simili mirabilia. Quanto al parente
è come non sia esistito mai. Aveva studiato
a Zurigo respinto in ogni materia
ma quando nel nostro paese le cose volgevano al peggio
crollava la testa a diceva eh a Zurigo a Zurigo . . .

Non so che senso abbia il ridicolo
nel tutto/nulla in cui viviamo ma
deve averne uno e forse non il peggiore.

SCHIAPPINO

Il figlio del nostro fattore
aveva fama di pessimo tiratore:
lo chiamavano Schiappa o con più grazia
Schiappino.
Un giorno si appostò davanti alla roccia
dove abitava il tasso in una buca.
Per essere sicuro del suo tiro
sovrappose al mirino una mollica di pane.
A notte alta il tasso tentò di uscire
e Schiappino sparò ma il tasso fece
palla di sé e arrotolato sparve
nella vicina proda. Non si vedeva a un passo.
Solo un tenue bagliore sulla Palmaria.
Forse qualcuno tentava di accendere la pipa.

Today there are no more greenhouses,
succulents or visitors,
nor the garden where such marvels could be seen.
As for my relative,
it's as though he never existed.
He had studied at Zurich and failed in every subject
but when things in our country took a turn for the worse
he'd shake his head and say, Ah, in Zurich, in Zurich . . .

I don't know the sense of the ridiculous
in the all-or-nothing we live in,
but it must have one and maybe not the worst.

BOOBY

The son of our farm manager
was known as a terrible shot:
they called him the Boob, or more graciously,
Booby.
One day he stationed himself in front of a hole
in the cliff where a badger lived.
To be sure of his aim
he put a crumb on his gunsight.
In the middle of the night the badger tried to come out
and Booby fired, but the badger
rolled up into a ball and disappeared
down the nearby bank. You couldn't see
a foot in front of you. Only a faint glow on the Palmaria.
Maybe someone was trying to light a pipe.

UNA VISITATRICE

Quando spuntava in fondo al viale
la zia di Pietrasanta noi ragazzi
correvamo a nasconderci in soffitta.
Il suo peccato: era vecchia e noiosa,
una tara che anche ai giovani di allora
pareva incomprensibile, insultante.
Mio padre l'abbracciava, dava ascolto
al fiume di disgrazie in cui la vecchiarda
nuotava come un pesce e poi faceva
scivolare due scudi nel borsetto
sempre aperto di lei. E infine le diceva
affréttati, tra poco arriverà
il trenino « operaio » che serve a te.
Non l'ho mai vista; oggi avrebbe assai più
di cento anni. Eppure quando leggo o ascolto
il nome PIETRASANTA penso ai pochi scudi,
al dolore del mondo, alla ventura-sventura
di avere un avo, di essere trisnipote
di chissà chi, di chi non fu mai vivo.

I NASCONDIGLI II

I

Il canneto dove andavo a nascondermi
era lambito dal mare quando le onde erano lunghe
e solo la spuma entrava a spruzzi e sprazzi
in quella prova di prima e dopo il diluvio.
Larve girini insetti scatole scoperchiate
a persino la visita frequente (una stagione intera)
di una gallina con una sola zampa.
Le canne inastavano nella stagione giusta
i loro rossi pennacchi; oltre il muro dell'orto
si udiva qualche volta il canto flautato

A VISITOR

When the aunt from Pietrasanta
appeared at the end of the avenue
we boys ran to hide in the attic.
Her sin: she was old and boring,
a flaw that even to the young back then
seemed incomprehensible, insulting.
My father hugged her, listened to
the stream of misadventures the old woman
swam in like a fish, and then
let a few coins slip into the purse
she always had open. Finally he said,
"Hurry, soon the little 'workers'' train
will be coming. You can take it."
I never saw her; today she'd be well over a hundred.
Yet when I read or hear
the name PIETRASANTA I think of those coins,
of the sorrow of the world, of the good/bad luck
of having an ancestor, of being the great-great-grandson
of who knows whom, of someone who never lived.

THE HIDING PLACES II

I

The canebrake where I went to hide
was lapped by the sea when the waves were long
and only the foam got in, in dribs and drabs,
in that rehearsal of before and after the deluge.
Larvae tadpoles insects tin cans without tops
even the frequent visits (one whole season)
of a hen with only one foot.
The canes sprouted their red plumes
in the proper season; beyond the garden wall
you could sometimes hear the flutelike song

del passero solitario come disse il poeta
ma era la variante color cenere
di un merlo che non ha mai (così pensavo)
il becco giallo ma in compenso esprime
un tema che più tardi riascoltai
dalle labbra gentili di una Manon in fuga.
Non era il flauto di una gallina zoppa
o di altro uccello ferito da un cacciatore?
Neppure allora mi posi la domanda
anche se una rastrelliera di casa mia
esibiva un fucile così detto a bacchetta,
un'arma ormai disusata che apparteneva
in altri tempi a uno zio demente.
Solo la voce di Manon, la voce
emergente da un coro di ruffiani,
dopo molti anni potè riportarmi
al canneto sul mare, alla gallina zoppa
e mi fece comprendere che il mondo era mutato
naturalmente in peggio anche se fosse assurdo
rimpiangere o anche solo ricordare
la zampa che mancava a chi nemmeno
se ne accorse e morì nel suo giuncheto
mentre il merlo acquaiolo ripeteva quel canto
che ora si ascolta forse nelle discoteche.

II

Una luna un po' ingobbita
incendia le rocce di Corniglia.
Il solito uccellino color lavagna
ripete il suo omaggio a Massenet.
Sono le otto, non è l'ora
di andare a letto, bambini?

OTTOBRE DI SANGUE

Nei primi giorni d'ottobre
sulla punta del Mesco
giungevano sfiniti dal lungo viaggio

50

of the solitary sparrow, as the poet called it
but this was the variant ash-gray blackbird
that never has a yellow beak (I thought)
but makes up for it by singing
a theme I later heard again
on the gentle lips of a Manon in flight.
Wasn't it the flute of a lame hen
or another bird felled by a hunter?
I didn't think about it then
though the gun-rack at my house
displayed a muzzle-loading rifle
an unused weapon that once
had belonged to a crazy uncle.
Only the voice of Manon, a voice emerging
out of a chorus of pimps
could bring me back after many years
to the canebrake by the sea and the lame hen
and make me understand the world had changed,
naturally for the worse, even if it was absurd
to regret or even remember
the missing foot she never knew was missing
who died in her bed of reeds
while the water-dipper rehearsed the song
which maybe you can hear in discotheques today.

II

A faintly gibbous moon
ignites the rocks of Corniglia.
The usual slate-colored bird
rehearses his homage to Massenet.
It's eight o'clock, isn't it time
to go to bed, children?

BLOODY OCTOBER

In the first days of October
the wood doves arrived
on the Point of Mesco, exhausted

i colombacci; e fermi al loro posto
con i vecchi fucili ad avancarica
imbottiti di pallettoni
uomini della mine e pescatori
davano inizio alla strage dei pennuti.
Quasi tutti morivano ma il giorno che ricordo
uno se ne salvò che già ferito
fu poi portato nel nostro orto.
Poteva forse morire sullo spiedo
come accade a chi lotta con onore
ma un brutto gatto rognoso
si arrampicò fino a lui e ne restò
solo un grumo di sangue becco e artigli.
Passione e sacrifizio anche per un uccello?
Me lo chiedevo allora e anche oggi nel ricordo.
Quanto al Mesco e alla Punta non ne è traccia
nel mio atlante scolastico di sessant'anni fa.

UN INVITO A PRANZO

Le monachelle che sul lago di Tiberiade
reggevano a fatica un grande luccio
destinato dicevano a Sua Santità
mi chiesero di restare qualora il Santo Padre
dichiarasse forfait (il che avvenne dipoi).
Non senza assicurarsi che sebbene at large
io ero un buon cattolico. Purtroppo
generose sorelle sono atteso al monte degli Ulivi
fu la risposta accolta da rimpianti
benedizioni e altro. Così ripresi il viaggio.
Sarebbe stato il primo luccio della mia vita
e l'ho perduto non so se con mio danno
o con vantaggio. Un luccio oppure un laccio?

by their long flight;
and motionless in place
aiming old muzzle-loaders stuffed with grapeshot
miners and fishermen
started the slaughter of the feathered kind.
Most of them died but on the day I'm recalling
one wounded bird escaped
and was brought into our garden.
Maybe he would have died on the spit,
as those who struggle honorably do,
but an ugly mangy cat
scrambled up to him and all that was left
was a clot of blood and the beak and claws.
Passion and sacrifice even for a bird?
I wondered then and, remembering, wonder now.
As for the Mesco and its Point, there's no trace
in my student atlas of sixty years ago.

AN INVITATION TO LUNCH

The nuns by Lake Tiberias who were having
trouble holding up a giant pike
they said was intended for His Holiness
asked me to stay in case the Holy Father
forfeited it (as he later did).
Not without making sure that though I was "at large"
I was a good Catholic. Unfortunately,
generous sisters, I'm expected at the Mount of Olives
was my answer, met with regrets,
blessings, etc. And so I went on my way.
It would have been the first pike of my life
and I lost it, I don't know whether to my harm
or advantage. A pike or a poke?

NEL DUBBIO

Stavo tenendo un discorso
agli « Amici di Cacania »
sul tema « La vita è verosimile? »
quando mi ricordai
ch'ero del tutto agnostico,
amore e odio in parti uguali e incerto
il risultato, a dosi alternate.
Poi riflettei ch'erano sufficienti
cinque minuti
due e mezzo alla tesi
altrettanti all'antitesi
e questo era il solo omaggio
possibile a un uomo senza qualità.
Parlai esattamente trentacinque secondi.
E quando dissi
che il sì e il no si scambiano le barbe
urla e fischi interruppero il discorso
e mi svegliai. Fu il sogno più laconico
della mia vita, forse il solo non sprovvisto
« di qualità ».

LA GLORIA O QUASI

A Ginevra alle felicemente defunte
Rencontres Internationales c'era una poltrona
sempre vuota e una scritta che diceva
Riservata alla vedova
di Affricano Spir.
Simili scritte appaiono sulle poltrone
di mezzo mondo
come apprendo da fogli autorevoli quali l'Eco
di Mazara del Vallo e il Diario de Pamplona.
Anche per me suppongo dev'essere scattata
tale macchinazione che non risparmia i celibi.

DOUBT

I was giving a lecture
to the "Friends of Cacania"
on the subject "Is Life Likely?"
when I remembered I
was totally agnostic,
love and hate in equal parts and the outcome
unsure, depending on the moment.
Then I decided five minutes
were enough—
two and a half for the thesis
two and a half for the antithesis
this was the only homage possible
for a man without qualities.
I spoke exactly thirty-five seconds.
And when I said
that yes and no were look-alikes
shouts and whistles interrupted my talk
and I awoke. It was the most laconic dream
of my life, maybe the only one not devoid
of "quality."

(SOMETHING LIKE) GLORY

In Geneva at the happily defunct
Rencontres Internationales there was an always-empty chair
with a note that said
Reserved for the Widow
of Afrikan Spir.
Similar notes appear on the chairs
of half the world
as I learn from reliable papers like the Echo
of Mazara del Vallo and the Diario de Pamplona.
I suppose like plans which don't spare bachelors
must have been hatched for me too.

Certo, Affricano, se la sua incredibile
consorte ch'ebbi il vanto di conoscere
lo avesse risparmiato, esulterebbe,
nichilista com'era in senso filosofico e non politico.
Non riuscì ad annullarsi. Oltre l'impresa
fallimentare della sua consorte
esistono dovunque quei monumentali
libri, le Enciclopedie che alla lettera S
portano un nome che anche senza di loro
a con scarsa sua gioia avrebbe galleggiato
alla meglio sul tempo.

Mi pare impossibile,
mia divina, mio tutto,
che di te resti meno
del fuoco rosso verdognolo
di una lucciola fuori stagione.
La verità è che nemmeno
l'incorporeo
può eguagliare il tuo cielo
e solo i refusi del cosmo
spropositando dicono qualcosa
che ti riguardi.

Non più notizie
da San Felice.

Hai sempre amato i viaggi
e alla prima occasione
sei saltata fuori
del tuo cubicolo.

Ma ora come riconoscersi
nell'Etere?

56

Surely, if Afrikan's incredible
consort whom I had the honor of knowing
had spared him, he would rejoice, nihilist that he was
in the philosophical, not the political sense.
He didn't manage to annul himself.
Apart from the disastrous doings of his wife
those monumental books are everywhere,
the Encyclopedias, which under the letter S
mention a name that even without them
would have managed, though with little joy,
to bob on the waves of time.

It seems impossible,
my divine one, my all,
that what remains of you
is less than the red-green spark
of a firefly out of season.
The truth is that not even
the immaterial
can approximate your heaven
and only the misprints of the cosmos
talking nonsense say something
that concerns you.

No more news
from San Felice.

You always loved travel
and at the first opportunity
you leapt
out of your cell.

But how to recognize each other
in the Ether?

Tergi gli occhiali appannati
se c'è nebbia e fumo nell'aldilà,
e guarda in giro e laggiù se mai accada
ciò che nei tuoi anni scolari fu detto vita.
Anche per noi viventi o sedicenti tali
è difficile credere che siamo intrappolati
in attesa che scatti qualche serratura
che metta a nostro libito l'accesso
a una più spaventevole felicità.
È mezzogiorno, qualcuno col fazzoletto
ci dirà di affrettarci perché la cena è pronta,
la cena o l'antipasto o qualsivoglia mangime,
ma il treno non rallenta per ora la sua corsa.

Il mio cronometro svizzero aveva il vizio
di delibare il tempo a modo suo.
E fu così
ch'erano solo le 5 e non le 6
quando potei sedermi al caffè San Marco.
Parve un'inezia, magari una fortuna
questo allungarsi dell'appuntamento
sebbene a lei pesasse assai l'attesa
ma il suo pallore divenne presto il mio.
Quale durata deve avere l'ultimo
(presumibile) addio? Non c'è manuale
di Erotica che illustri degnamente
la scomparsa di un dio. In tali eventi
che il cronometro avanzi o retroceda
non conta nulla.

Wipe your misty glasses
if there's haze or smoke in the beyond,
and look around and down and see if it ever occurs,
what was called life in your student years.
For us too, the living or so we say,
it's hard to believe we're trapped,
waiting for some lock to spring
and make a more terrifying
happiness available on demand.
It's midday, someone with a handkerchief
will tell us to hurry, lunch is ready,
lunch or antipasto or whatever fodder,
but for now the train won't slow its course.

My Swiss watch had the tic
of sampling time on its own.
And so it was
that it was only 5 not 6
when I sat down at the Caffè San Marco.
It seemed nothing, or even good luck,
this prolonging of our appointment,
except that the wait weighed heavily on her;
but her pallor soon became mine.
How long will it last, the final
(presumable) farewell? There's no Sex Manual
that rightly illustrates
the disappearance of a god. In such cases
whether the watch goes forward or back
makes no difference.

LUNI E ALTRO

1938

Arrestammo la macchina
all'ombra di alcune rovine.
Qui sarà sbarcata la jeunesse dorée
e dopo secoli vi sostò Gabriel
per compiervi la pessima delle sue prove.
Più modesti dobbiamo contentarci
di poco: il Poveromo, la Fossa dell'Abate.
Troppe cose, dicesti. Ne ho abbastanza
di cadaveri illustri.
                    E ripartimmo
senza nessuna nostalgia: quel poco
che ancora oggi resiste.

                                        a C.

Ho tanta fede in te
che durerà
(è la sciocchezza che ti dissi un giorno)
finché un lampo d'oltremondo distrugga
quell'immenso cascame in cui viviamo.
Ci troveremo allora in non so che punto
se ha un senso dire punto dove non è spazio
a discutere qualche verso controverso
del divino poema.

So che oltre il visibile e il tangibile
non è vita possibile ma l'oltrevita
è forse l'altra faccia della morte
che portammo rinchiusa in noi per anni e anni.

Ho tanta fede in me
e l'hai riaccesa tu senza volerlo
senza saperlo perché in ogni rottame

LUNI, ETC.

1938

We stopped the car
in the shade of some ruins.
Here the jeunesse dorée debarked
and centuries later Gabriel stopped
to suffer the worst of his trials.
More modest, we must be content
with little: the Poor Man, the Abbot's Ditch.
Too much, you said. I have enough
illustrious corpses.
                    And we took off
without the slightest nostalgia: the little
that still survives today.

                                        to C.

I have such faith in you
that it will last
(this is the foolishness I told you once)
until a flash from beyond destroys
the immense waste heap in which we live.
We'll find ourselves then in I don't know what place
if it makes sense to say place where there's no space
discussing certain controversial verses
of the divine poem.

I know beyond the visible and tangible
no life is possible, but the life beyond
may be the other face of death
that we carried locked inside us for years and years.

I have such faith in me
and you rekindled it not meaning to
or knowing, for in every wreck in life down here

della vita di qui è un trabocchetto
di cui nulla sappiamo ed era forse
in attesa di noi spersi e incapaci
di dargli un senso.

Ho tanta fede che mi brucia; certo
chi mi vedrà dirà è un uomo di cenere
senz'accorgersi ch'era una rinascita.

CLIZIA DICE

Sebbene mezzo secolo sia scorso
potremo facilmente ritrovare
il bovindo nel quale si stette ore
spulciando il monsignore delle pulci.
Sul tetto un usignolo si sgolava
ma non ebbe successo. Quanto al gergo
delle sagre del popolo o a quello
delle commedie o farse vive solo
in tradizioni orali, se con noi fosse
come un giorno un maestro del sermone umile
nonché del bronzeo della patrologia,
tutto sarebbe facile. Ma dove
sarà quel giorno e dove noi?
Se esiste un cielo e in esso molte lingue,
la sua fama d'interprete salirebbe
in altri cerchi ancora e il puzzle sarebbe
peggiore che all'inferno di noi sordomuti.

CLIZIA NEL '34

Sempre allungata
sulla chaise longue
della veranda

there's a trap door we know nothing of
and maybe it was waiting for us
who were lost and unable
to give it a meaning.

I have such faith that it burns me; surely
he who sees me will say, He's a man of ashes,
not recognizing this was a rebirth.

CLIZIA SAYS

Though half a century is gone
it will be easy for us to find
the bay window where we sat for hours
defleaing the monsignor of the fleas.
On the roof a nightingale sang himself hoarse
without success. As for the slang
of the popular festivals
or the comedies or farces that only survive
in the oral tradition, everything would be easy
if we had with us, as we did one day,
a master of common speech
not to mention the bronze one of the Patrology.
But where will that day be, and where will we?
If there's a heaven, and many tongues in it,
his fame as an interpreter would rise
into still other orders and the "puzzle"
would be worse than in the inferno of us deaf mutes.

CLIZIA IN '34

Still lounging
on the chaise longue
of the veranda

che dava sul giardino,
un libro in mano forse già da allora
vite di santi semisconosciuti
e poeti barocchi di scarsa reputazione
non era amore quello
era come oggi e sempre
venerazione.

PREVISIONI

Ci rifugiammo nel giardino (pensile se non sbaglio)
per metterci al riparo dalle fanfaluche
erotiche di un pensionante di fresco arrivo
e tu parlavi delle donne dei poeti
fatte per imbottire illeggibili carmi.
Così sarà di me aggiungesti di sottecchi.
Restai di sasso. Poi dissi dimentichi
che la pallottola ignora chi la spara
e ignora il suo bersaglio.
                                Ma non siamo
disse C. ai baracconi. E poi non credo
che tu abbia armi da fuoco nel tuo bagaglio.

INTERNO/ESTERNO

Quando la realtà si disarticola
(seppure mai ne fu una) e qualche sua parte
s'incrosta su di noi
allora un odore d'etere non di clinica
ci avverte che la catena s'è interrotta
e che il ricordo è un pezzo di eternità

facing the garden
a book in hand, perhaps already then
the lives of half-unheard-of saints
and baroque poets of scant reputation
this wasn't love
then as now it was always
veneration.

PREDICTIONS

We escaped into the garden (hanging if I'm correct)
to hide from the erotic
chitchat of a new boarder
and you spoke about poets' women
created to pad unreadable odes.
So it will be with me, you added under your breath.
I was still as stone. Then I said, You forget
the bullet doesn't know who's firing it
and doesn't know its target.
                                    But we're not
in a shooting gallery, said C. And besides
I don't believe you have firearms in your luggage.

INSIDE/OUTSIDE

When reality comes undone
(if ever there was one) and some of its parts
encrust themselves on us
then an odor of ether not from a clinic
alerts us that the chain has been broken
and the memory is a piece of eternity

che vagola per conto suo
forse in attesa di rintegrarsi in noi.
È perciò che ti vedo
volgerti indietro dall'imbarcadero
del transatlantico che ti riporta
alla Nuova Inghilterra.
oppure siamo insieme nella veranda
di « Annalena »
a spulciare le rime del venerabile
pruriginoso John Donne
messi da parte i deliranti abissi
di Meister Eckhart o simili.
Ma ora squilla il telefono e una voce
che stento a riconoscere dice ciao.
Volevo dirtelo, aggiunge, dopo trent'anni.
Il mio nome è Giovanna, fui l'amica di Clizia
e m'imbarcai con lei. Non aggiungo altro
né dico arrivederci che sarebbe ridicolo
per tutti e due.

NEL '38

Si era con pochi amici
nel Dopopalio
e ci fermammo per scattare
le foto d'uso.
Ne ho ancora una, giallo sudicia,
quasi in pezzi,
ma c'è il tuo volto incredibile,
meraviglioso.
Si era nel '38.
Più tardi dissero
che bordeggiavi « a sinistra »
ma la notizia non mi sorprese
perché sapevo che l'Essere
non ha opinioni o ne ha molte

66

wandering on its own
maybe waiting to reform itself in us.
So I see you
turning away from the dock
on the ocean liner that will carry you
to New England
or we're together on the veranda
of "Annalena"
defleaing the rhymes of the reverend
itchy John Donne
having set aside the dizzying voids
of Meister Eckhart and company.
But now the telephone rings
and a voice I can barely recognize says hello.
I wanted to call, it adds, after thirty years.
My name is Giovanna, I was Clizia's friend
and I sailed with her. I have nothing to add
not even arrivederci, which would be ridiculous
for us both.

IN '38

We were with a few friends
after the Palio
and stopped to take
the usual photos.
I still have one, a dirty yellow
practically in shreds
but there it is, your incredible face,
miraculous.
This was in '38.
Later they said
you tacked to the "left"
but hearing it didn't surprise me
for I knew that Existence
has no opinions or many

a seconda del suo capriccio
e chi non può seguirle
ne è inseguito.
Si era nel '38.

QUARTETTO

In una istantanea ingiallita
di quarant'anni fa
ripescata dal fondo di un cassetto
il tuo volto severo nella sua dolcezza
e il tuo servo d'accanto; e dietro Sbarbaro
briologo e poeta – ed Elena Vivante
signora di noi tutti: qui giunti per vedere
quattro ronzini frustati a sangue
in una piazza-conchiglia
davanti a una folla inferocita.
E il tempo? Quarant'anni ho detto e forse zero.
Non credo al tempo, al big bang, a nulla
che misuri gli eventi in un prima e in un dopo.
Suppongo che a qualcuno, a qualcosa convenga
l'attributo di essente. In quel giorno eri tu.
Ma per quanto, ma come? Ed ecco che rispunta
la nozione esecrabile del tempo.

« POICHÉ LA VITA FUGGE . . . »

Poiché la vita fugge
e chi tenta di ricacciarla indietro
rientra nel gomitolo primigenio,
dove potremo occultare, se tentiamo
con rudimenti o peggio di sopravvivere,

according to its whim
and he who can't follow them
is followed by them.
This was in '38.

FOURSOME

In a yellowed snapshot
of forty years ago
fished out of the bottom of a drawer
your face, severe in its sweetness
and your servant beside you; and Sbarbaro behind—
bryologist and poet—and Elena Vivante
the mistress of us all: come here to see
four nags in a shell-shaped piazza
whipped till they bled
in front of a frenzied crowd.
And the date? I said forty years, it may be zero.
I don't believe in time, the big bang, or anything
that measures events in a before and after.
I suppose someone, something, deserves
the epithet of being. On that day it was you.
But for how long, but how? And here again
the execrable idea of time resurfaces.

"SINCE LIFE IS FLEEING . . ."

Since life is fleeing
and he who tries to set it in reverse
gets caught in the primordial web again,
where can we hide, if we try to survive
with rudiments or worse,

gli oggetti che ci parvero
non peritura parte di noi stessi?
C'era una volta un piccolo scaffale
che viaggiava con Clizia, un ricettacolo
di Santi Padri e di poeti equivoci che forse
avesse la virtù di galleggiare
sulla cresta delle onde
quando il diluvio avrà sommerso tutto.
Se non di me almeno qualche briciola
di te dovrebbe vincere l'oblio.

E di me? La speranza è che sia disperso
il visibile e il tempo che gli ha dato
la dubbia prova che questa voce È
(una E maiuscola, la sola lettera
dell'alfabeto che rende possibile
o almeno ipotizzabile l'esistenza).
Poi (sovente hai portato
occhiali affumicati e li hai dimessi
del tutto con le pulci di John Donne)
preparati al gran tuffo.
Fummo felici un giorno, un'ora un attimo
e questo potrà essere distrutto?
C'è chi dice che tutto ricomincia
eguale come copia ma non lo credo
neppure come augurio. L'hai creduto
anche tu? Non esiste a Cuma una sibilla
che lo sappia. E se fosse, nessuno
sarebbe così sciocco da darle ascolto.

CREDO

1944

Forse per qualche sgarro nella legge
del contrapasso
era possibile che uno sternuto in via Varchi 6 Firenze
potesse giungere fino a Bard College N. J.

the objects that seemed
an undying part of ourselves?
Once there was a little bookcase
that traveled with Clizia, a receptacle
for Holy Fathers and questionable poets;
may it have the power to float
on the crest of the waves
when the flood has drowned everything.
If nothing of me, at least some bit of you
ought to vanquish oblivion.

And as for me? The hope is that the visible
will dissolve, along with time, which gave it
the dubious proof that this voice Exists
(a capital E, the only letter in the alphabet
that makes existence possible
or at least a possible hypothesis).
Then (you often wore
dark glasses but put them aside
for good with the fleas of John Donne)
prepare for the big dive.
We were happy for a day, an hour, an instant
and can this be destroyed?
Some say everything begins again
just like a copy but I don't believe it
not even as a wish. Did you
believe it too? There's no sibyl at Cumae
who knows. And if there were,
no one would be foolish enough to listen.

CREDO

1944

Maybe it was through some loophole in the law
of retribution
that a sneeze in Via Varchi, 6, in Florence
got as far as Bard College, N.Y.

Era l'Amore? Non quello che ha popolato
con un orrendo choc il cielo di stelle e pianeti.
Non tale la forza del dio con barba e capelli
che fu detronizzato dai soci del Rotary Club
ma degno di sopravvivere alle loro cabale.
Credo vero il miracolo che tra la vita e la morte
esista un terzo status che ci trovò tra i suoi.
Che un dio (ma con la barba) ti protegga
mia divina. Ed il resto, le fandonie
di cui siamo imbottiti sono meno
che nulla.

A CLAUDIA MUZIO

Eravate sublime
per cuore e accento,
il fuoco e il ghiaccio fusi
quando Qualcuno disse basta
e fu obbedito.
Ovviamente
non fu affar vostro la disubbidienza
ma questo non ci conforta, anzi infittisce
il mistero: che sia pronto a dissolversi,
ciò che importa, ma tardo e incancellabile
l'essere per cui nascere fu un refuso.

« QUANDO LA CAPINERA . . . »

Quando la capinera fu assunta in cielo
(qualcuno sostiene che il fatto
era scritto nel giorno della sua nascita)
certo non si scordò di provvedersi

Was it Love? Not the love whose terrifying shock
peopled the heavens with stars and planets.
No such power in the god with beard and hair
dethroned by the membership of the Rotary Club,
though he deserves to survive their cabals.
I believe it's true, the miracle that between life and death
a third state exists that found us among its own.
May a god (but a god with a beard) protect you,
my divine one. And the rest, the little lies
we're stuffed with, are less
than nothing.

TO CLAUDIA MUZIO

You were sublime
in heart and diction
fire and ice combined
when Someone said, Enough
and was obeyed.
Obviously
disobedience wasn't your business
but this is no comfort, it only deepens the mystery:
that the being for whom birth was a misprint
is ready to dissolve,
which is what matters, but late and indelible.

"WHEN THE BLACKCAP . . ."

When the blackcap was assumed into heaven
(some maintain that this fact
was inscribed on the day of its birth)
it certainly didn't forget to bring

di qualche amico del suo repertorio
scelto tra i più fidati, Albert Savarus
e la piccola Alice strappata dal suo Wonderland.
Per il primo non sono problemi
ma per l'altra
distolta dall'ombrello del suo fungo
non mancherà qualche dissidio: ch'io
sappia tra i micologi del cielo
è buio pesto.

CARA AGLI DEI

Vista dal nostro balcone
in un giorno più chiaro d'una perla
la Corsica appariva sospesa in aria.
È dimezzata dicesti come spesso
la vita umana.
Le vieillard s'approcha, il avait
bien cinquante ans
dissi citando Rousseau, non si saprà mai
quanto deve durare una vita. Non sapevo
allora che tu per tuo conto
avresti risolto il problema
scacciandone una parte: « un barba! ».
Non so ancora se fui caro o discaro agli Dei
e quale di queste Maschere abbia ragione o torto.
Il avait bien 50 ans! Quello ch'è sottinteso
in quel bien potrebbe anche farmi impazzire.

UNA VISITA

Roma 1922

Quasi a volo trovai una vettura
lasciando l'hôtel Dragoni.
Ci volle non poco tempo per giungere al cancello

74

some friends from its repertory
choosing from among the most trusted Albert Savarus
and little Alice, snatched from her Wonderland.
For the first there's no problem
but the other
stolen from the umbrella of her mushroom
will suffer some discomfort: from what I hear
among the mycologists of heaven
it's pitch black.

BELOVED OF THE GODS

Seen from our balcony
on a day brighter than a pearl
Corsica seemed hung in the air.
It's cut in half you said
the way human life often is.
Le vieillard s'approcha, il avait
bien cinquante ans
I said quoting Rousseau, we'll never know
how long a life will last. I didn't know then
that for yourself
you would solve the problem
by getting rid of one part: "Old bore!"
I still don't know if I was loved by the gods or not
or which of these masks is right or wrong.
Il avait bien 50 ans! What's implied
in that bien could very well drive me mad.

A VISIT

Rome 1922

Practically flying I found a cab
leaving the Hotel Dragoni.
It took no little time to reach the gate

dove lei mi attendeva. Dentro erano i parenti
e gl'invitati. Le signore in lungo
gli uomini in nero o nerofumo
io solo in grigio. C'erano due ammiragli
omonimi, il prefetto, due ex ministri
molto loquaci. Si parlò di tutto,
con preferenza per guerre da fare o prendere.
Io e lei quasi muti.
Venne servito il tè coi buccellati
di Cerasomma. E noi sempre meno loquaci.
Dopodiché allegai che fosse per me tempo
« di togliere il disturbo » e non trovai obiezioni.
Permetti
che ti accompagni disse lei uscendo dal suo mutismo.
Ma era ormai per poco, col cancello vicino.
Sulla ghiaia il suo passo pareva più leggero.
Non tardò una vettura.
                              Hasta la vista dissi
facendomi coraggio. La sua risposta si fuse
con uno schiocco di frusta.

POSTILLA A « UNA VISITA »

Certo non fu un evento degno di storia
quel primo mio viaggio a Roma. Ma la storia
anche la privatissima storia di Everyman
registra ben altre sciocchezze. Non sa che farsene
di due cuori neppure infranti (e se anche
lo fossero o lo furono?). La storia è disumana
anche se qualche sciocco cerca di darle un senso.

where she was waiting. Her family
and the guests were inside. The ladies in gowns
the men in black or charcoal,
only I was in gray. There were two admirals
with the same name, the prefect, and two very chatty
ex-ministers. They talked about everything,
preferably wars to make or take.
She and I were practically mute.
Tea was served with cakes
from Cerasomma. And we said less and less.
After which I allowed it was time for me
"to remove my disturbance" and I met no objections.
Let me
show you the way, she said, coming out of her silence.
But now time was short, with the gate so close.
On the gravel her step seemed to lighten.
A cab lost no time in appearing.

                              Hasta la vista, I said

taking courage. Her answer got mixed
with the crack of the whip.

NOTE ON "A VISIT"

Certainly it wasn't a happening worthy of history
that first trip of mine to Rome. But history
even the intimate history of Everyman
records many another foolishness. It doesn't know what to do
with two hearts that weren't even broken (and what if
they had been, what if they were?). History is inhuman
even if certain fools try to give it a meaning.

AH!

Amavi le screziature le ibridazioni
gli incroci gli animali
di cui potesse dirsi mirabil mostro.
Non so se nel collège di Annecy
qualcuno abbia esclamato vedendoti e parlandoti
con meraviglia Ah! E fu da allora
che persi le tue tracce. Dopo anni seppi
il peggio. Dissi Ah! e tentai di pensare ad altro.
Rari i tuoi libri, la Bibbia
e il Cantico dei Cantici,
un bosco per la tua età
con tanto di cartello cave canem,
qualche romanzo del Far West e nulla
che fosse scritto per l'infanzia e i suoi
confini così incerti. Tuttavia,
se tu fossi scomparsa allora, anche a te
non sarebbe mancato un tenerissimo
Ah!
Ma più tardi nessuno
o soltanto il buon Dio quale che fosse
accompagnò la tua vacanza con un Ah!
che dicesse stupore o smarrimento.
Forse qualcuno si fermò sull'A
che dura meno e risparmia il fiato.
Poi fu silenzio. Ora l'infante là
dove si sopravvive se quella è vita
legge i miei versi zoppicanti, tenta
di ricostruire i nostri volti e incerta dice
Mah?

AH!

You loved markings crossbreedings
crossroads animals
that could be called miraculous monsters.
I don't know if in the school at Annecy
someone seeing and talking to you exclaimed, Ah!
in wonder. After that I lost track of you.
Years later I learned the worst.
I said, Ah! and tried to think of something else.
You had few books, the Bible
and the Song of Songs,
a grove for your youth
with a big sign that said cave canem,
a few Westerns
and nothing written for childhood
with its so uncertain boundaries. Still,
if you had disappeared then
there would have been a very tender
Ah!
for you too. But later
no one or only the good Lord such as he was
answered your absence with an Ah!
that said stupefaction or bewilderment.
Maybe somebody stopped at the A
which is shorter and saves breath.
Then there was silence. Today the child
there where life goes on if that is life
reads my limping lines, tries
to reconstruct our faces, and uncertain says
Ah?

UNCOLLECTED

POEMS

Poesie disperse

ELEGIA

Non muoverti.
Se ti muovi lo infrangi.
È come una gran bolla di cristallo
sottile
stasera il mondo:
e sempre più gonfia e si leva.
O chi credeva
di noi spiarne il ritmo e il respiro?

Meglio non muoversi.
È un azzurro subacqueo
che ci ravvolge
e in esso
pullulan forme imagini rabeschi.
Qui non c'è luna per noi:
più oltre deve sostare:
ne schiumano i confini del visibile.

Fiori d'ombra
non visti, imaginati,
frutteti imprigionati
fra due mura,
profumi tra le dita dei verzieri!
Oscura notte, crei fantasmi o adagi
tra le tue braccia un mondo?

Early Poems, 1918-1928

ELEGY

Don't move.
If you move you'll shatter it.
The world is like a great bubble
of fragile
crystal this evening:
swelling, swelling and rising.
Oh, who among us thought
that we could watch its rhythm and its breathing?

Better not move.
It's a subaqueous blue
that enfolds us
and within it swarm
forms images arabesques.
Here there's no moon for us:
it must halt far beyond,
a foaming at the edges of the visible.

Shadow-flowers,
unseen, imagined,
orchards locked
between two walls,
perfumes among the fingers of the greenery!
Dark night, do you make ghosts, or do you lay
a world within your arms?

Non muoverti.
Come un'immensa bolla
tutto gonfia, si leva.
E tutta questa finta realtà
scoppierà
forse.
Noi forse resteremo.
Noi forse.
Non muoverti.
Se ti muovi lo infrangi.

Piangi?

MONTALE IN GUERRA

a Solmi

Desiderio di stringer vecchie mani
di rispecchiarsi in visi un tempo noti
sotto il grondare di un gelato azzurro
che la campana dello Schrapnell scuote.

MUSICA SILENZIOSA

I

Minuetto di sensazioni
lietezza e insieme dolore,
giorni che tu vorresti
tanto che non vuoi nulla
e si trastulla
coi resti
di vecchie enciclopediche ambizioni
il cuore.

Don't move.
Like a giant bubble
everything swells and rises.
And all this sham reality
will burst
maybe.
Maybe we'll be staying.
Maybe.
Don't move.
If you move you'll shatter it.

Are you crying?

MONTALE AT WAR

to Solmi

The desire to shake old hands again
to see oneself in faces once known well
under the dripping of an icy blue
that vibrates to the shrapnel's knell.

SILENT MUSIC

I

Minuet of sensations
joy and sadness together
days when you want so much
you want nothing
and the heart
plays games
with the remains
of old encyclopedic ambitions.

Facezie inezie illusioni?
Una piuma un nonnulla un bibelot
non so
di che ti componi
minuetto di sensazioni.
Basta un carro che passi rombando per la strada
a renderti, e ne piangi, imagine di un mondo
che cada.

2

Minuetto di sensazioni
sfiorar di un'ala che si alza,
e tu non sai, non t'opponi
al tempo che t'incalza,
triste e gaio minuetto
suonato
non si sa dove e spesso per dispetto
stuonato.

Dolcezze tristezze
fantasie?
Ciò che si volle e non si compirà,
chi sa
di che ti componi
minuetto di sensazioni.

Minuetto irrequieto che t'alzi, che corri nel mondo
qualcuno c'è che indovina il tuo senso amaro
profondo,
minuetto di malinconia giunto alle nostre porte
stamane così lento che sembri l'elegia
di tutte le speranze nate morte.

Jokes stupidities illusions?
A feather a nothing a toy
I don't know
what you're made of
minuet of sensations.
A carriage rumbling in the streets is all
it takes to bring you—and it makes you cry—
the image of a world about to fall.

2

Minuet of sensations
graze of a wing that rises
and you don't know, you don't resist
the time that's trailing you
sad, gay minuet
played
who knows where and often, out of envy,
out of tune.

Sweetnesses sadnesses
imaginings?
What was wished for and won't come to be.
Who knows
what you're made of,
minuet of sensations.

Restless minuet that rises and runs through the world
someone divines your bitter, deep intent
minuet of melancholy
come to our doors so slow this morning
that you seem the elegy
of every hope that is stillborn.

A GALLA

Chiari mattini,
quando l'azzurro è inganno che non illude,
crescere immenso di vita,
fiumana che non ha ripe né sfocio
e va per sempre,
e sta – infinitamente.

Sono allora i rumori delle strade
l'incrinatura nel vetro
o la pietra che cade
nello specchio del lago e lo corrùga.
E il vocìo dei ragazzi
e il chiacchiericcio liquido dei passeri
che tra le gronde svolano
sono tralicci d'oro
su un fondo vivo di cobalto,
effimeri . . .

Ecco, e perduto nella rete di echi,
nel soffio di pruina
che discende sugli alberi sfoltiti
e ne deriva un murmure
d'irrequieta marina,
tu quasi vorresti, e ne tremi,
intento cuore disfarti,
non pulsar più! Ma sempre che lo invochi,
più netto batti come
orologio traudito in una stanza
d'albergo al primo rompere dell'aurora.
E senti allora,
se pure ti ripetono che puoi
fermarti a mezza via o in alto mare,
che non c'è sosta per noi,
ma strada, ancora strada,

e che il cammino è sempre da ricominciare.

FLOATING

Bright mornings,
when the blue is a deceit that doesn't fool,
immense expansion of life,
torrent wtih no banks, no mouth
that runs forever
and stays—unendingly.

Now there are the noises in the streets
the crack in the glass
or the rock that falls
in the mirror of the lake and furrows it.
And the shouting of the boys
and the liquid chatter of the sparrows
fluttering in the eaves
are trellises of gold
on a living cobalt ground,
ephemeral . . .

Look, and lost in the net of echoes,
in the breath of frost
that falls on the thinned trees
and draws from them
a murmur of restless shore
you could almost, and it makes you quiver,
fervent heart, dissolve,
and not go on! But always when you plead for this
you beat stronger,
like a clock misheard in a hotel room
at the first breaking of dawn.
And you feel then,
even if they keep saying you can halt
halfway, or on the sea,
that there's no rest for us,
only street, more street,

and always the journey to begin again.

SUONATINA DI PIANOFORTE

Vieni qui, facciamo una poesia
che non sappia di nulla
e dica tutto lo stesso,
e sia come un rigagnolo di suoni
stentati
che si perde tra sabbie
e vi muore con un gorgoglio sommesso;
facciamo una suonatina di pianoforte
alla Maurizio Ravel,
una musichetta incoerente
ma senza complicazioni,
ché tanto credi proprio
a grattare nel fondo non c'è senso;
facciamo qualche cosa di « genere leggèro ».

Vieni qui, non c'è nemmeno bisogno
di disturbar la Natura
co' i suoi seriosi paesaggi
e le pirotecniche astrali;
né tireremo in ballo
i grandi problemi eterni,
l'immortalità dello Spirito
od altrettali garbugli;
diremo poche frasi comunali
senza grandi pretese,
da gente ormai classificata,
gente priva di « profondità »;
e se le parole ci mancheranno
noi strapperemo il filo del discorso
per svagarci
in un minuetto approssimativo
che si disciolga in arabeschi d'oro,
si rompa in una gran pioggia di lucciole
e dispaia lasciandoci negli occhi
un pullulare di stelle, un'ossessione di luci.

PIANO SONATINA

Come, let's make a poem
that tastes of nothing
and says everything the same,
and let it be like a brook of troubled
sounds
that loses itself in the sands
and dies there gurgling softly;
let's make a sonatina for piano
à la Maurice Ravel,
a little piece of music, incoherent
but uncomplicated,
since really, believe me,
there's no sense in digging deep;
let's make "something light."

Come here, there's no need
to bother Nature,
with its serious landscapes
and starry pyrotechnics;
nor shall we bring to bear
the great eternal problems,
the immortality of the Soul
or other conundrums;
we'll say a few commonplaces
with no great pretensions,
like people already labeled,
people without "profundity";
and if words fail us
we'll break the chain of the argument
to amuse ourselves
in an approximate minuet
which will dissolve in golden arabesques,
break into a great rain of fireflies
and disappear, leaving us
with a swarm of stars in our eyes, obsessed with lights.

Poi quando la suonatina languirà davvero
la finiremo come vuole la moda
senza perorazioni urlanti ed enfasi;
la finiremo, se ci parrà il caso,
nel momento in cui pare ricominciare
e il pubblico rimane con un palmo di naso.

La spegneremo come un lume, di colpo. Con un soffio.

ACCORDI

(Sensi e fantasmi di una adolescente)

I

VIOLINI

Gioventù troppe strade
distendi innanzi alle pupille
mie smarrite:
quali si snodano, erbite,
indecise curve in piane tranquille,
quali s'avventano alla roccia dura
dei monti,
o ad orizzonti vanno ove barbaglia
la calura!
Sono qui nell'attesa di un prodigio
e le mani mi chiudo nelle mani.
Forse è in questa incertezza,
mattino che trabocchi
dal cielo,
la più vera ricchezza e tu ne innimbi
tutto che tocchi!
Occhi corolle s'aprono
in me – chissà? – o nel suolo:
tutto vaneggia e nella luce nuova
volere non so più né disvolere.
Solo
m'è dato nel miracolo del giorno,
o cuore fatto muto,

Then when the sonatina grows truly faint
we'll end it as fashion dictates
without roaring perorations or pomposity;
we'll end it, if it seems right,
just when it seems to be starting again
and the audience's nose is out of joint.

We'll put it out like a flame, in a flash. With a breath.

CHORDS

(Feelings and fantasies of an adolescent girl)

I

VIOLINS

Youth, you lay out
too many streets
before my bewildered eyes;
some unravel, grassy,
indecisive curves in quiet plains;
some run up to the hard rock
of the mountains,
or go to the horizons where the heat
dazzles!
I'm here waiting for a miracle
clasping my hands.
Maybe in this uncertainty,
morning brimming over from the sky,
lies the truest wealth
and with it you enhalo
everything you touch!
Eyes, blossoms, open
in me—who knows—or the earth:
everything drifts and in the new light
I no longer know desire or non-desire.
Still
it is given to me in the miracle of the day,
O heart struck dumb,

scordare gioie o crucci,
ed offrirti alla vita
tra un mattinare arguto
di balestrucci!

2
VIOLONCELLI

Ascolta il nostro canto che ti va nelle vene
e da queste nel cuore ti si accoglie,
che pare, angusto, frangersi: siamo l'Amore, ascoltaci!
Ascolta il rosso invito del mattino
che rapido trascorre come ombra d'ala in terra;
assurgi dal vivaio dei mortali
d'opaca creta, ignari d'ogni fiamma,
e seguici nel gurge dell'Iddio
che da sé ci disserra,
echi della sua voce, timbri della sua gamma!
Come l'esagitato animo allora
esprimerà scintille che giammai
avresti conosciute! La tua forma
più vera non capisce ormai nei limiti
della carne: t'è forza di confonderti
con altre vite e riplasmarti tutta
in un ritmo di gioia; la tua scorza
di un dì, non t'appartiene più. Sarai
rifatta dall'oblio, distrutta dal ricordo,
creatura d'un attimo. E saprai
i paradisi ambigui dove manca
ogni esistenza: seguici nel Centro
delle parvenze: (ti rivuole il Niente!).

3
CONTRABBASSO

Codesti i tuoi confini: quattro pareti nude,
da tanti anni le stesse;
e in esse
un susseguirsi monotono di necessità crude.

94

to forget joys and sorrows
and offer you to life
in a morning bright
with martins!

2

CELLOS

Hear our song, which travels in your veins
and through them is drawn into your heart,
which, narrow, seems to break: hear us, we are Love!
Hear the red invitation of the morning
which runs like a wing's shadow on the ground;
rise up from the storehouse of the mortals
made of dull clay, who never felt a flame,
and follow us into the river of light of God
from whom we spring,
his voice's echoes, his scale's tones!
Then how the tormented mind
will give off sparks that you have never known!
Your truest form
is held no longer by the limits of the flesh:
you have the power to fuse with other lives
and totally regenerate
in a rhythm of joy; your former husk
is yours no longer. You will be
remade by oblivion, destroyed by memory,
creature of an instant. And you'll know
the dubious heavens in which all being
is missing: follow us to the Core
of appearances: (the Void wants you again!).

3
DOUBLE BASS

These are your boundaries: four naked walls
the same year after year:
and within them one unending stretch
of raw necessities.

Invano con disperate ali la tua fantasia corre tutto
il fastoso dominio della vita universa;
non uscirai tu, viaggiatrice spersa,
dai limiti del « Brutto » ...

4
FLAUTI-FAGOTTI

Una notte, rammento, intesi un sufolo
bizzarro
che modulava un suo canto vetrino.
Non v'era luna: e pure quella nota
aguzza e un poco buffa siccome una
fischiata d'ottavino
illuminava a poco a poco il parco
(così pensavo) e certo nel giardino
le piante in ascoltarla
si piegavano ad arco
verso il terreno ond'ella pullulava;
e a questa ciarla
s'univano altre, ma più gravi, e come
bolle di vetro luminose intorno
stellavano la notte che raggiava.
Di contro al cielo buio erano sagome
di perle,
grandi flore di fuochi d'artifizio,
cupole di cristallo e nel vederle
gli occhi s'abbacinavano
in un gaio supplizio!
Esitai un istante: indi balzai
alla finestra e spalancai le imposte
sopra la vasca sottostante; e tosto
fu un tuffarsi di rane canterine,
uno sciacquare un buffo uno svolìo
d'uccelli nottivaghi;
ed improvviso
uscì da un mascherone di fontana
che gettava a fior d'acqua il suo sogghigno,
uno scroscio di riso
soffocato in un rantolo

In vain with desperate wings does your imagination travel
the whole sumptuous realm of universal life;
you will not escape, strayed voyager,
the confines of the "Dismal" . . .

4
FLUTES, BASSOONS

One night, I remember,
I heard a weird tin whistle
playing its glassy song.
There was no moon: yet that sharp note,
a bit ridiculous
like the shrill of a piccolo,
little by little lit the park
(or so I thought) and clearly in the garden
the plants on hearing it
bent in an arc
toward the spot that it was budding from
and this chatter
was joined by others, but deeper,
and like bubbles of luminous glass all around
they lit up the radiant night.
They were the shapes
of pearls against the dark sky,
great flowers of fireworks,
crystal cupolas, and seeing them
my eyes went blind
in joyful torment!
I hesitated an instant: then I leapt
to the window and threw open the shutters
over the pool: and instantly
there was a diving of singing frogs
a rinsing squalling fluttering
of night-flying birds;
and suddenly
from the great mask of a fountain
casting its grin on the water
came a burst of laughter
suffocated by a hoarse

roco
che l'eco ripeté
sempre più fioco.

E allora il buio si rifece in me.

5
OBOE

Ci son ore rare
che ogni apparenza dintorno vacilla s'umilia scompare,
come le stinte
quinte
d'un boccascena, ad atto finito, tra il parapiglia

I sensi sono intorpiditi,
il minuto si piace di sé;
e nasce nei nostri occhi un po' stupiti
un sorriso senza perché.

6
CORNO INGLESE

Il vento che stasera suona attento
– ricorda un forte scotere di lame –
gli strumenti dei fitti alberi e spazza
l'orizzonte di rame
dove strisce di luce si protendono
come aquiloni al cielo che rimbomba
(Nuvole in viaggio, chiari
reami di lassù! D'alti Eldoradi
malchiuse porte!)
e il mare che scaglia a scaglia,
livido, muta colore
lancia a terra una tromba
di schiume intorte;
il vento che nasce e muore
nell'ora che lenta s'annera
suonasse te pure stasera
scordato strumento,
cuore.

death rattle
which the echo repeated
fainter and fainter.

And then the darkness was remade in me.

5
OBOE

There are rare moments
when all appearances around us waver, decline, disappear
like the faded
screens
of a stage set, in the turmoil, when the play's over.

The senses are numb,
the moment is pleased with itself;
and in our eyes, a bit amazed
a smile begins for no reason.

6
ENGLISH HORN

The wind that plays alert tonight
—recalling a sharp clash of swords—
the instruments of the thick trees and sweeps
the copper horizon
where stripes of light stretch out
like kites in the sky which roars
(Traveling clouds, bright kingdoms
up above! High Eldorados'
half-shut doors!)
and the livid sea which scale by scale
changes colors
tosses ashore
a trumpet of twisted spume;
the wind that is born and dies
in the hour that slowly goes dark
if only it could play you too tonight,
untuned instrument,
heart.

7

Stamane, mia giovinezza,
una fanfara in te squilla,
voce di bronzo che immilla
l'eco, o disperde la brezza.

Vedi letizia breve, molto attesa,
ch'entri nella mia vita, tutta cinta
di fiori, come sia per te la pésa
malinconia dei giorni andati vinta!

O primavera fuggevole, vedi come gli animi invasi
dal tuo respiro si plachino, si facciano gli occhi sereni,
e per te in cielo s'accampino, di là dai torbidi occasi,
arcobaleni!

(Unissono fragoroso d'istrumenti. Comincia lo spettacolo della Vita).

Qui dove or è molti anni
s'espresse il nostro mattino
s'invera la tua vita
Guido, in un'ora che sembra
dolcisonante risacca
di memorie su dolci prode.
Bellezza dell'arco che si tende
e di tutto che ascende nel ronzante
tripudiare del sole! Io non un fiore
t'offro, sì questa bacca.
Conservala com'è; che nulla teme.
Su lei su te Acquario mai non versi
l'urne; sopra le viaggino
tersi gli astrali segni!

7
BRASSES

This morning, my youth,
a fanfare blazes in you,
a voice of bronze the echo
makes a thousand, or the breeze undoes.

You see, brief happiness so long awaited,
that comes into my life all girdled with flowers,
how thanks to you the weighty
sadness of the old days is defeated!

O fleeting spring, you see how souls invaded
by your breath are appeased, how clear their eyes become,
how for you they camp in the sky, beyond the cloudy horizons,
rainbows!

(Resonant unison of instruments. The spectacle of Life begins.)

Here where many years ago by now
our morning spoke itself
your life moves into the true,
Guido, in an hour that seems
like a sweet-sounding washing-back
of memories on sweet shores.
Beauty of the arc that stretches,
beauty of all that rises in the humming
exultation of the sun! I offer you
no flower, just this cone.
Keep it as it is; for it fears nothing.
On it, on you, may Aquarius never
empty his urn; above it may
the scoured star-signs fly.

LETTERA LEVANTINA

Vorrei che queste sillabe
che con mano esitante di scolaro
io traccio a fatica per voi,
vi giungessero in un giorno d'oscura
noia; quando il meriggio
non rende altra parola
che quella d'una gronda che dimoia;
e in noi non resiste una sola
persuasione al minuto che róde,
e i muri candidi ci si fanno incontro
e l'orrore di vivere sale a gola.

Per certo vi sovverrete allora
del compagno di tante ore passate
nelle vie lastricate di mattoni,
che tagliano, seguaci a infossamenti e ascese,
i nostri colli nani cui vestono le trine
rade di spogli rami.
E vi parrà di correre non più sola
sotto i dòmi arruffati degli olivi
tra abbrivî e brusche soste,
come rimpiccinita in un baleno.
O il ricordo vi si farà pieno
degli alberi che abbiamo conosciuti,
e rivedrete le barbate palme
ed i cedri fronzuti,
o i nespoli che tanto amate.

Questo è il ricordo di me che vorrei porre
nella vostra vita:
essere l'ombra fedele che accompagna
e per sé nulla chiede;
l'imagine ch'esce fuori da una stampa tarmata,
scordata memoria d'infanzia, e crea un istante di pace
nella convulsa giornata.
E delle volte se una forza ignota
vi regge in un groviglio
di brucianti ore,

LEVANTINE LETTER

I'd like these syllables
which with a hesitant scholar's hand
I trace laboriously for you
to reach you on a day of dark
boredom; when the noon
gives out no other word
than the one a drain makes as it thaws;
and not a single belief in us
resists the minute that gnaws,
and the white walls rise up against us
and the fear of living rises in the throat.

Surely you'll remember then
your comrade of so many bygone hours,
on the brick-paved ways that rise and fall
cutting our stunted hills
dressed in the scant lace
of bare branches.
And you'll feel you no longer run alone
under the ruffled domes of the olive trees,
starting and suddenly stopping,
as if in a flash you were small again.
Oh, your memory will fill
with the trees we knew,
and you'll see the bearded palm again
and the fronded cedars,
or the medlars you love so well.

This is the memory of me I'd like to make
a part of your life:
to be the faithful shadow that goes with you
and asks nothing for itself;
the image that stands out from a moth-eaten etching,
a lost childhood memory, and brings a moment of peace
in the frenzied day.
And sometimes if an unknown force
holds you in a maze
of scorching hours,

oh illudervi poteste
che v'ha preso per mano alcuni istanti
nel segreto,
non l'Angelo dei libri edificanti
ma il vostro amico discreto!

Ascoltate ancora, voglio svelarvi qual filo
unisce le nostre distanti esistenze
e fa che se voi tacete io pure v'intendo, quasi
udissi la vostra voce che ha ombre e trasparenze.
Un giorno mi diceste della vostra infanzia
scorsa framezzo ai cani e alle civette
del padre cacciatore; ed io pensai che foste
permeata da allora dell'essenza
ultima dei fenomeni, radice
delle piante frondose della vita.
Così mentre le eguali
vostre inconscie nei giuochi
trapassavano i giorni, o tra le vane
cure del mondo, ignave,
i vostri pochi Autunni,
amica, sì puri di stigmate,
scorgevano già dell'enigma
che ci affatica, la Chiave.

Anch'io sovente nella mia rustica
adolescenza levantina
salivo svelto prima della mattina
verso le rupestri cime che s'inalbavano;
e m'erano allato
compagni dal volto bruciato dal sole.
Zitti stringendo nei pugni
annosi archibugi,
col fiato grosso s'andava nel buio;
o si sostava, a momenti,
per misurare a dita
la polvere nera e i veccioni
pestati in fondo alle canne.
Attendevo affondato in un cespuglio
che la lunga corona
dei colombi selvatici

oh, if you could make yourself believe
that for a few moments he's taken your hand
in secret,
not the Angel of the edifying books
but your discreet friend!

Listen again, I want to uncover the thread
that unites our distant beings
so that if you're silent I still understand, almost
as if I heard your voice with its shadows and transparencies.
One day you told me about your girlhood,
spent with the dogs and little owls
of your hunter father; and I thought
you were imbued from then on with the ultimate
essence of phenomena, the root
of the luxuriant plant of life.
So while your unknowing
playmates spent their days
in games or, lazily,
in the empty cares of the world,
your few Autumns, friend,
so free of pains,
already were aware of the enigma
that troubles us, the Key.

I too, often in my rural
Levantine adolescence,
climbed quickly before morning
to the whitening rocky heights;
beside me were playmates
with sunburned faces.
Silent, holding ancient
muskets in our hands,
panting, we went in the dark;
or stopped sometimes
to measure with a finger
the black powder and buckshot
we packed deep down in the barrels.
I waited hidden in a thicket
for the long circle
of wild pigeons

salisse dalle vallette
fumide degli uliveti
volta al cacume, ora adombrato ed ora
riassolato, del monte.
Lentamente miravo il capo-fila
grigio sopravanzante, indi premevo
lo scatto; era la bòtta nell'azzurro
sécca come di vetro che s'infrange.
Il colpito scartava, dava all'aria
qualche ciuffo di piume, e scompariva
come un pezzo di carta in mezzo al vento.
D'attorno un turbinare d'ali pazze
e il sùbito rifarsi del silenzio.

E ancora appresi in quelle mie giornate
prime, guardando
il lepre ucciso nelle basse vigne
o il cupreo scoiattolo che reca
la coda come una torcia
rossa da pino a pino,
che quei piccoli amici della macchia
portano a lungo talvolta
nel cuoio i pallini minuti
d'antiche sanate ferite
prima che un piombo più saldo
li giunga a terra per sempre.

Forse divago; ma perché il pensiero
di me e il ricordo vostro mi ridestano
visioni di bestiuole ferite;
perché non penso mai le nostre vite
disuguali
senza che il cuore evòchi
sensi rudimentali
e imagini che stanno
avanti del difficile
vivere ch'ora è il nostro.
Ah intendo, e lo sentite
voi pure: più che il senso
che ci rende fratelli degli alberi e del vento;
più che la nostalgia del terso

to rise from the steaming
valleys of olives
toward the mountaintop, now in shadow
now in sun.
Slowly I watched their gray
leader break away, then pulled
the trigger; there was a sharp clap
in the blue, like shattering glass.
Then the hit bird fell, gave the air
a few tufts of feathers and disappeared
like a sheet of paper in the wind.
Around, a storm of crazy wings
and the sudden return of silence.

And again I'd learned in those
first days of mine, as I watched
the hare killed in the low vineyards
or the copper-colored squirrel that holds
its tail up like a red torch
from pine to pine,
that those little friends in the thicket
can sometimes carry for years
the buckshot from old healed wounds
deep in their hides
until more solid lead
brings them to earth for good.

Maybe I digress; but that's because
thinking of me and remembering you awakens
visions of little wounded animals;
because I never think of our
disparate lives
but my heart evokes
old rudimentary feelings
and images that stand out
from the difficult life
that is ours now.
Oh, I know it, and you feel it too:
more than the feeling
that makes us brothers to the trees and wind;
more than the nostalgia for the clean sky

cielo che noi serbammo nello sguardo;
questo ci ha uniti antico
nostro presentimento
d'essere entrambi feriti
dall'oscuro male universo.

Fu il nostro incontro come un ritrovarci
dopo lunghi anni di straniato errare,
e in un attimo il guindolo del Tempo
per noi dipanò un filo interminabile.
Senza sorpresa camminammo accanto
con dimesse parole e volti senza maschera.
Penso ai tempi passati
quando un cader di giorno o un rifarsi di luce
mi struggevano tanto
ch'io non sapevo con chi mai spartire
la mia dura ricchezza, e pure intorno
di me sentivo fluire una potenza
benevolente, sorgere impensato
fra me e alcun altro un fermo sodalizio.
Intendo ch'eravate già al mio fianco
in quegli istanti; che vi siete ancora,
se pur lontana, in questo giorno stanco
che finisce senza apoteosi;
e che insieme guardiamo biancheggiare
tra i marosi e le spesse brume
le scogliere delle Cinqueterre
flagellate dalle spume.

Scendiamo la via che divalla
tra i grovigli dei dumi;
ci guiderà il volo di una farfalla
in faccia agli orizzonti rotti dai fiumi.

that we kept in our look;
this has kept us together,
our ancient sense
of having both been wounded
by the dark universal ill.

Our meeting was like finding each other
after long years of estrangement and wandering,
and in an instant the reel of Time
unwound an endless thread for us.
Unsurprised, we walked side by side
with simple words and faces without masks.
I think of the past
when the end of a day or the return of light
made me yearn so
that I never knew with whom to share
my raw wealth, and yet around me
I felt a benevolent power was flowing,
a solid pact was being forged
unplanned between me and another.
I know you were already at my side
in those moments; that you are there still,
though distant, on this tired day
that ends without apotheosis;
and that together we are watching
the reefs of the Cinque Terre whiten
lashed by the surf
among the breakers and thick mists.

Let's go down the road that slopes
among tangles of brambles;
we'll know the way from the flight of a butterfly
against the horizons broken by streams.

Serriamoci dietro come una porta
queste ore di esitanze e di groppi in gola.
Nostalgie non dette che più c'importano?
Anche l'aria d'attorno ci vola!

Ed ecco che a uno svolto ci appare
di colpo la riga argentea del mare;
buttano ancora l'àncora le nostre vite anèle.
Ne intendo il tonfo – Addio, sentiero! Ed ora
mi sento tutto fiorito non so se d'ali o di vele . . .

Sotto quest'umido arco dormì talora Ceccardo.
Partì come un merciaio di Lunigiana
lasciandosi macerie a tergo.
Si piacque d'ombre di pioppi, di fiori di cardo.

Lui non recava gingilli: soltanto un tremulo verso
portò alla gente lontana
e il meraviglioso suo gergo.
Andò per gran cammino. Finché cadde riverso.

GABBIANI

Ali contr'ali ondanti biancogrigie,
frullanti spole nel giro degli occhi,
croci rotanti all'aria che le porta.
È deserta la foce, affondato
il sole, ogni voce s'ammorta.
Meno pesanti giungono i rintocchi.
Li tiene uno sbattìo di sbarrate ali.

Let's lock behind us like a door
these hours of hesitations and lumps in the throat.
Unspoken nostalgias—what do they matter anymore?
Even the air around us is flying away!

And see at a turn how suddenly
the silver stripe of the sea appears;
our yearning lives lift anchor once again.
I hear the splash—Pathway, farewell. And now I feel
I'm sprouting wings all over, or are they sails? . . .

Ceccardo slept under this damp arch sometimes.
He set out like a Lunigiana peddler
leaving wreckage behind.
He loved the shade of poplars and thistle blossoms.

He didn't carry junk: just the quavering line
that he brought to the faraway folk,
and his marvelous jargon.
He went the great route. Until he fell on his back.

GULLS

Wings against wings gray/white in waves
shuttles beating in the field of vision,
crosses whirling in the air that lifts them.
The river mouth is empty, the sun
has sunk, and every voice has died.
The bells come back less heavily.
What muffles them is a beating of stretched wings.

Ali ed ali contro al nascimento
dei lumi nell'ora chiara ancora,
sciamar d'esseri volti all'avvento
d'un'astrale scintillante flora.
Ali ali ali morbida tomba
al tuo finire, fratello:
oh ti cullino come il mare un burchiello!
L'onda più sulla piaggia non rimbomba.

NEL VUOTO

La criniera del sole s'invischiava
tra gli stecchi degli orti e sulla riva
qualche pigra scialuppa pareva assopita.

Non dava suono il giorno
sotto il lucido arco
né tonfava
pigna o sparava boccio
di là dai muri.

Il silenzio ingoiava tutto,
la nostra barca non s'era fermata,
tagliava a filo la sabbia, un segno a lungo
sospeso in alto precipitava.

Ora la terra era orlo che trabocca,
peso sciolto in barbaglio,
la vampa era la spuma dell'oscuro,
il fosso si allargava, troppo fondo
per l'àncora e per noi
                    finché di scatto
qualcosa avvenne intorno, il vallo chiuse
le valve, tutto e nulla era perduto.

Wing upon wing against the birth
of lights in the still-bright hour,
swarm of beings turned toward the coming
of an astral scintillating flower.
Wings wings wings, my brother,
gentle tomb for your end:
oh, may they rock you like a rowboat on the sea!
The wave no longer thunders on the sand.

IN THE VOID

The sun's mane was infiltrating
among the brambles of the garden and on the shore
a few lazy sloops seemed dazed.

The day gave off no sound
under the shining arc
and no cone dropped
no bud was bursting
beyond the walls.

The silence was engulfing everything,
our boat was not yet still,
it cut a line in the sand, a sign
long hung above began to fall.

The earth now was an overflowing brim
a weight released in dazzle,
the blaze was the foaming of the dark,
the ditch was widening, too deep
for the anchor and us
              then suddenly
something happened around us, the lock's
valves closed, all and nothing was lost.

Ed io fui desto al suono del tuo labbro
ritrovato – da allora prigionieri
della vena che attende nel cristallo
la sua giornata.

Buona Linuccia che ascendi
la via nella vita, esitante,
e temi il tempo che incrina,
l'acqua che varca i ponti e va distante.
Rammento Miramare perlato, rammento
il boschetto in salita d'onde appare
l'arsenale e il suo fumo che si confonde
con la malinconica nebbia mattutina.
Rammento le tue parole a ventaglio,
aperte-chiuse con scorrevole grazia,
e l'adriatica sera che disperdeva
la tua curiosità insazia.

Rammento . . .
                Nulla più rammento. Quanto
tempo, quanta distanza, quante mura
dritte; e che inferno attorno, scatenato.

Dolci anni che di lunghe rifrazioni
illuminano i nostri ultimi, sommersi
da un fiotto che straripa,
anni perduti quando l'avventura
era la stipa
coronata di voli in giro al campo
o un lubrico guizzare di tarantola
su screpolate mura;

And I awoke at the sound of your
rediscovered voice—both of us prisoners from now on
of the vein that waits in the crystal
for its hour.

Good Linuccia, climbing up
the pathway into life, who hesitates
and fears the time about to crack,
the water that passes the bridge and flows away.
I remember pearled Miramare, I remember
the grove on the way up where you see
the arsenal and its smoke that mixes
with the melancholy morning mist.
I remember your fanlike words,
open-and-shut with flowing grace,
and the Adriatic evening that appeased
your insatiable curiosity.

I remember . . .
                    nothing else. So much
time, such distance, so many tall
walls: and around us, what a raging hell.

Sweet years whose long refractions
illuminate our last ones, drowned
in a flood that overflows,
lost years when adventure was
a swarming crowned
with flights around the field
or the slippery darting of a lizard
on cracked walls;

dolci anni che ravviso come poca
luce tra nebbia ora che intorno mi ardono
senza vampa, infinito
struggersi che più e più borea rinfoca,
volti e pensieri ch'io non so e riguardo
sbigottito,
anni che seguirà nella vicina
bara colei che vede e non intende
quando la tragga il gorgo che mulina
le esistenze e le scende
nelle tenebre.

pour Mme. Gerti T. F.
1er fragment

. . .

Par toi nos destinées d'antan sont refondues
comme ces plombs, Gerti, dans la cuiller creuse

sur l'étoile blême du gaz; par toi je peux
plonger dans l'eau mes jours perdus, les voir

sur un papier, hérissés ou plats comme une semelle
restée au bord de la route; le jour s'achève,

l'année s'en va, ma vie n'existe, j'ai bien
la cravate grise au lieu de la cravate rouge,

et ne suis pas sauvé; par toi, j'entends
les Grandes-Voix-Eternelles qu'en moi déferlent . . .

sweet years I look back on like a little light
in the haze, now that they burn around me
flameless, an endless
failing the north wind more and more excites,
faces and thoughts that I don't recognize
and watch dismayed,
years that she who sees and doesn't understand
will follow in the nearby bier
when the eddy brings her down
that whirls existences and sinks them
into the shade.

for Mme. Gerti T. F.
1st fragment

. . .

You say our destinies of yesteryear have been recast
like these leads, Gerti, in the empty spoon

on this pale star of gas; you say that I
can plunge my lost days in the water, see them

bristling on paper, or flat, like a sole
beside the road; the day is ending,

the year is passing, my life does not exist,
I have the gray tie, not the red,

and am not saved; you say I hear
the Great-Eternal-Voices that unfurl in me . . .

VENTAGLIO PER S.F.

L'epitalamio non è nelle mie corde,
la felicità non fu mai la mia Musa,
la sposa l'ho vista appena, un attimo, tra le sàrtie
di un trealberi giunto dal reo Norte
all'Isola. Il mio augurio è dunque « a scatola chiusa ».

Per lei, ma non per me, perché *la boîte à surprise*
è fatta per chi col suo nome decapitò Cassandra.
Le gemma che v'è nascosta, frutto di un'inaudita
mainmise del bene sul male, io l'ho chiamata Speranza.

LA MADRE DI BOBI

Una fiaba narrava che Trieste
fosse crocicchio o incontro di culture.
Forse era vero, un tempo; ma neppure
io lo sapevo quando
vi giunsi, il '19, mezzo fante
e mezzo pellegrino. Solo dopo,
nell'inamena via che porta il nome
di Cecilia Rittmeyer, una querula madre
legata a triplo filo a un figlio in fuga
mi aprì al suo Genio, a quel dio dispotico
e indifferente che poi l'ha lasciata.

Later Poems, 1962-1977

FAN FOR SANDRA F.

The epithalamium is not among my chords,
happiness was never my Muse,
the bride I barely saw, for an instant, among the shrouds
of a three-master come down from the evil North to the Island.
My wish is therefore something "sight unseen."

For her, but not for me, for the *boîte à surprise*
is made for the one whose name beheaded Cassandra.
The jewel that's hidden inside, the fruit of an unheard-of
mainmise of good over evil, I've called Hope.

BOBI'S MOTHER

The story went that Trieste
was a crossroads or meeting-place of cultures.
It may have been so once upon a time;
but I didn't know it
when I arrived in '19, half-soldier,
half-pilgrim. Only later,
in the desolate street named for
Cecilia Rittmeyer, did a querulous mother
triply bound to a son in flight
open the door on her Genius,
that despotic, indifferent god who later left her.

Oggi pensarla è una tortura: quasi
frugare in una piaga che credevo
rimarginata.

REFRAIN DEL PROFESSORE-ONOREVOLE

Il problema del full time mi preoccupa
ben poco.
Non lumi chiedono i pupilli, ma
il coprifuoco.

LA BELLE DAME SANS MERCI II

Se l'uomo è fatto vivere dalla sua causa
e l'atto dal motivo
non si torna alle origini, si vive
una retrocessione senza arresti.
Di te, del tuo segreto ho cercato invano
l'archetipo vivente o estinto, quale che fosse.
Tra gli animali forse l'unicorno
che vive nelle insegne araldiche e non oltre.
Per me non c'era dubbio: io ero il tasso,
quello che s'appollottola e piomba dalla cresta
alla proda tentando di sfuggire
al pennello da barba, il suo traguardo.
Non per te questo scorno, Pilar, se
il nome che tu porti ha ancora un senso.

Thinking of her today is torture;
like digging into a wound I thought
had healed.

REFRAIN OF THE HONORABLE PROFESSOR

The problem of full-time is my least
preoccupation.
My pupils ask for curfew,
not illumination.

LA BELLE DAME SANS MERCI II

If man is kept alive by his cause
and the act by its motive
there's no return to origins, we live
an unending regression.
For you, for your secret, I've sought in vain
the living or extinct archetype, whatever it was.
Among animals maybe the unicorn,
alive on heraldic shields and nowhere else.
For me there was no doubt: I was the badger,
who rolls into a ball and sinks from the crest
to the shore, trying to escape
the shaving-brush, his end.
No such ignominy for you, Pilar,
if the name you bear still has a meaning.

POSTILLA

Forse non sarà il caso di vedersela.
L'autopsia della vita non fu più
che l'illusione di due o tre centurie.
Viverla è altro percorso, altro binario.

ALTRA POSTILLA

... o forse il nuovo dio
ha messo in pensione l'Altro
e non ci ha neppure avvertiti.
Non so, non oso credere che il nuovo
sia stato così scaltro
da insinuarsi alla furtiva. Noi
fummo ciechi, non lui. Moltiplicando gli occhi
siamo rimasti al buio.

IL 3

La fortuna del 3
non è opera del diavolo.
L'uno è la solitudine
il due la guerra
e il 3
salva la capra
e i cavoli.

FOOTNOTE

It may be we won't see to it.
The autopsy of life was nothing more
than the illusion of two or three hundred.
Living's another journey, another track.

SECOND FOOTNOTE

. . . or maybe the new god
has retired the Other
and hasn't even warned us.
I don't know. I don't dare believe the new one
is shrewd enough to sneak in furtively.
It was we who were blind, not he.
Multiplying our eyes
we remained in the dark.

THE 3

The luck of the 3
isn't the devil's work.
One is loneliness
two is war
and 3
means having your cake
and eating it too.

PRECAUZIONI

Non a torto
mi avevano raccomandato,
se andavo a cena dal diavolo,
di usare il cucchiaio lungo.
Purtroppo
in quelle rare occasioni
il solo a disposizione
era corto.

PICCOLO DIARIO

Sono infreddato, tossicchio
è lo strascico dell'influenza,
domani andrò a ricevere
una medaglia per benemerenze
civiche o altre che ignoro.
Verrà a prendermi un tale
di cui non so più il nome. Ha una Mercedes,
presiede un Centro Culturale (quale?).

* * *

Si accumula la posta
« inevasa » sul tavolo. Parrebbe
che io sia molto importante
ma non l'ho fatto apposta.
Dio mio, se fosse vero
che mai saranno gli altri?

* * *

Comunicare, comunicazione,
parole che se frugo nei miei ricordi
di scuola non appaiono. Parole
inventate più tardi,
quando venne a mancare anche il sospetto
dell'oggetto in questione.

PRECAUTIONS

Not incorrectly
they had advised me
to use the long spoon
if I went to dine with the devil.
Unfortunately
on those rare occasions
the only one available
was short.

LITTLE DIARY

I have a cold, a cough,
it's the tail end of the flu,
tomorrow I go to receive
a medal for civic
good deeds or others I don't know about.
Someone will come for me
whose name I no longer remember. He has a Mercedes,
directs a Cultural Center (which?).

* * *

The mail is piling up
"unanswered" on the table. It would seem
I am very important
but I didn't do it on purpose.
My God, if it were true,
what would other people be?

* * *

Communication, communiqués,
words that if I search in my schoolboy
memories don't appear.
Words invented later,
when even the notion of the object in question
had vanished.

VERSO LODI

Era una bella giornata di primavera.
Sul tardi ci fermammo al quagliodromo,
un torrone di uccelli senza vuoti o interstizi
sotto una luce accecante.
Erano in molti nel gabbione e tranquilli,
forse un milione o più. E non mancavano
di nulla. Non toccati dal bacillo
dell'istruzione.

LA COMMEDIA

Si discute sulla commedia:
se dev'essere un atto unico o in tre o in cinque
come il genere classico;
se a lieto fine o tragico; se sia
latitante l'autore o reperibile
o se un'équipe lo abbia destituito;
se il pubblico pagante e gli abusivi,
onorevoli o altro
non stronchino i soppalchi dell'anfiteatro;
se sulla vasta udienza calerà
un sonno eterno o temporaneo; se
la pièce debba esaurire tutti i significati
o nessuno;
si arguisce che gli attori non siano necessari
e tanto meno il pubblico; si farfuglia dai perfidi
che la stessa commedia sia già stata
un bel fiasco e ora manchino i sussidi
per ulteriori repliche; si opina
che il sipario da tempo è già calato senza
che se ne sappia nulla; che il copione
è di un analfabeta ed il sovrintendente
non è iscritto al partito. Così si resta in coda

NEAR LODI

It was a beautiful spring day.
On the late side we stopped at the rifle range,
a tower of birds without holes or slats
under a blinding light.
They were a great many in the cage, and quiet,
maybe a million or more. And they lacked
for nothing. Uninfected by the germ
of instruction.

THE DRAMA

We're discussing the drama:
should it be one act or three or five
as it is classically;
should it have a happy or sad ending;
should the author hide out or be available
or has a team deposed him;
will the paying (and nonpaying) public
honorable or otherwise
crack the mezzanines of the amphitheater;
will an eternal or momentary sleep
fall on the vast audience; should
the piece exhaust all its meanings
or none;
it's argued actors aren't necessary
much less the public; there's mumbling by the faithless
that the play itself has already been a big
fiasco and now there are no subsidies
for more performances; it's been suggested
that the curtain rang down long ago
without anyone knowing; that the script
is by an illiterate and the director
doesn't belong to the party. And so we stand in line

al botteghino delle prenotazioni
in attesa che lo aprano. O vi appaia
il cartello ESAURITO.

SI SLOGGIA

Anche senza volerlo mi disloco.

Invidio la cicogna che se va
sa dove va e dove tornerà.

LEGGENDO IL GIORNALE

I dialoghi tra gli atei
e i credenti
si sono svolti, dicono,
senza incidenti.
Solo un po' stanchi i glutei
per le lunghe sedute
e conversioni reciproche,
imprevedute
restando eguali, com'era prevedibile,
le percentuali.

La poesia consiste,
nei suoi secoli d'oro,
nel dire sempre peggio
le stesse cose. Di qui l'onore e il pregio.
In tempi magri è un'epidemia,

waiting for the box office
to open. Or for a sign
that says Sold Out.

MOVING

Not even wanting to, I get displaced.

I envy the stork who goes,
knows where's he's going and where he's returning.

READING THE PAPER

The talks between the atheists
and believers
took place, they say,
without incident.
Only the buttocks got a little tired
from all the sitting
and the mutual, unforeseen
conversions,
though the percentages, predictably,
remained unchanged.

Poetry throughout
its golden ages has consisted
in saying the same things
worse and worse. Hence its honor and prestige.
In lean times it's an epidemic,

chi non l'ha avuta l'avrà presto, ma
ognuno crede che la malattia
sia di lui solo e che all'infermeria
il posto per l'egregio sia il peggiore.

Rabberciando alla meglio
il sistema hegeliano
si campa da più di un secolo.
E naturalmente invano.

La trascendenza è in calo, figuriamoci!
L'immanenza non vale una castagna secca.
La via di mezzo è il denaro. Meglio
cercare altrove.

* * *

E la follia? Anche lei per i suoi pregi
ma non pei fatti; solo per gli egregi.

* * *

E questi egregi sarebbero
davvero usati dal gregge?
Su questo punto urge
un decreto-legge.

Per me
l'ago della bilancia
sei sempre tu.
M'hanno chiesto chi sei. Se lo sapessi
lo direi a gran voce. E sarei chiuso
tra quelle sbarre donde non s'esce più.

whoever hasn't had it will get it soon,
but each believes the sickness is his alone
and that in the infirmary
the place for the first will be the worst.

For longer than a century
they've been trying to repair
Hegel's system, naturally
not getting anywhere.

Imagine, transcendence is down!
Immanence isn't worth a fig.
Money's the middle way.
Better shop around.

* * *

And madness? It too, for its quality
but not its reality; only for the outstanding.

* * *

And the outstanding, are they really
used by the masses?
This point calls
for a new set of laws.

For me
you're still
the needle of the scales.
They asked me who you are. If I knew
I'd shout it out. And I'd be shut
behind bars we don't escape from.

AL VIDEO

Luna che obtorto collo
guardo in fotografia
quale fortuna t'incolse
quando ti distaccasti
da una terra in ammollo.

Ma ora?

OBIEZIONI

Il Creatore fu increato? Questo
può darsi ma è difficile pensarlo
imprigionati
come siamo nel tempo e nello spazio.
E se non fu increato, anzi diventa
tardivamente opera nostra, allora
tutto s'imbroglia. Siamo Dio, a miliardi,
anche i poveri e i pazzi e ora soltanto
ce ne accorgiamo? E poi, con quanta voglia?

SURROGATI

Le violenze, i pestaggi,
le guerre (ma locali, che non ci tocchino),
gli allunamenti, d'interesse sempre
descrescente,
le lotterie, le canzonette, il calcio
internazionale,
tutto questo è l'ersatz della terza e ultima
(sempre ultima, s'intende,
per gli allocchi)
catastrofe mondiale?

ON THE SCREEN

Moon I see in the photo
face turned away
what fate befell you
when you withdrew
from a world at sea?

But now?

OBJECTIONS

Was the Creator uncreated? This may be
but it's difficult to think so
trapped
as we are in time and space.
And if not uncreated, he becomes
belatedly our work, and then
everything's confused. Are we God, in the billions,
even the poor and crazy and only now
discovering it? And if so, how happily?

SUBSTITUTES

Violence, beatings,
wars (but local ones, that don't concern us),
moon-landings, of ever lesser
interest,
lotteries, pop songs, inter-
national soccer,
is all this the ersatz of the third and final
(always final, of course,
for the foolish)
world catastrophe?

I NUOVI CREDENTI (?)

I capelloni ignorano
di inventare una nuova religione.
È più oscura delle altre ma sappiamo
che il peggio non ha limiti e come strada
è la più larga e sicura.
I capelloni suonano
trapani casseruole e scacciacani.
Il vecchio dio è un po' sordo: li preferisce
ai migliori complessi americani.
Il vecchio dio sa che non può guidare
il suo gregge con fulmini o rampogne.
Sordo, non cieco, sa che la vergogna deve
traboccare dov'è. E quanto al resto
se la vedranno gli altri. È troppo presto
(troppo tardi) per lui.

IL VATE

Ha prenotato un letto di prima classe
nel treno che va e non torna dall'aldilà.
Non porta con sé bagagli ma solo il fascicoletto
dei suoi morceaux choisis con l'autorevole
soffietto di . . . di . . . di . . . Forse lassù
farà il suo effetto.

L'insonnia fu il mio male e anche il mio bene.
Poco amato dal sonno mi rifugiai nella veglia.
nel buio che non è poi tanto nero
se libera i fantasmi dalla luce
che li disgrega. Non sono tanto grati
questi ospiti notturni ma ce n'è uno
che non è sogno e forse è il solo vero.

THE NEW BELIEVERS (?)

The hippies don't know
they've invented a new religion.
It's more obscure than the others but we know
that the worst is boundless and as a way
it's the widest and safest.
The hippies play
on drills, casseroles and toy
pistols. The old god's a little deaf;
he prefers them to the best American bands.
The old god knows he can't direct
his flock with lightning or rebukes.
Deaf but not blind, he knows that shame
must break out where it exists. And others
will see to the rest. It's too soon
(too late) for him.

THE PROPHET

He's reserved a first-class sleeping compartment
in the train that doesn't come back from the beyond.
He's carrying no baggage, just the little book of his select
sayings with the impressive
blurb of ... of ... of ... Maybe up above
it will have an effect.

My insomnia was trouble but it also did me good.
Little loved by sleep, I fled to waking
into the dark, which isn't so black after all
if it frees the ghosts from the light
that keeps them apart. They're not so welcome,
these nocturnal guests, but there's one
who isn't a dream, and may be the only real one.

IL DONO

Chi ha il dono dell'umore
può disprezzare la vita?
Questa vita, sia pure, ma non è la sola,
non è la sola vita
dei fatti nostri, delle nostre parole.
E forse non è vita
neppure quella dell'aldilà
secondo la proposta antropomorfica
che dà barba e capelli al pantocratore
e le civetterie del superstar.
Noi non sappiamo nulla ma è ben certo
che sapere sarebbe dissoluzione
perché la nostra testa non è fatta per questo.
Solo ci è noto che non è sapere
l'escogitazione,
quella che fa di noi i più feroci animali,
ma un dono che ci fu dato
purché non se ne faccia uso
e nemmeno si sappia di possederlo.
Ed è un sapere mutilo, inservibile,
il solo che ci resta nell'attesa
come in sala d'aspetto che giunga il treno.

VANILOQUIO

La scomparsa del mondo che manda al settimo cielo
sinistri questuanti non m'interessa per nulla.
Sembra che sia lontana, per ora non minacciosa.
Inoltre c'è il pericolo che la notizia sia falsa.
Falsa o vera è scomparsa rateale.
E la mia quota? Forse ne ho già pagata
qualche rata e per le altre posso attendere.
« Ma fia l'attender corto »? O maledette

THE GIFT

Can the man with the gift of humor
disdain life?
Call it this life, but it's not the only one,
it's not the only life
of our acts, our words.
And maybe the one beyond
isn't life either
according to the anthropomorphic theorem
which gives the pantocrator a beard and hair
and the coyness of a superstar.
We know nothing but it's very clear
that knowing would mean dissolving
since our brain isn't made for this.
All we've seen is that cogitation
which makes us the most ferocious animal
isn't knowing,
but a gift that was given us
provided we not use it
or even know we have it.
And it's a maimed, unserviceable knowledge,
all that's left for us who wait
as in a waiting room for the train to arrive.

IDLE CHATTER

The disappearance of the world that sends sinister mendicants
to the seventh heaven doesn't interest me at all.
It seems far off, not threatening for now.
And there's the danger the news may be false.
True or false, it's a disappearance by installments.
And my monthly rate? Maybe I've already made
some payments and can wait for the others.
"But may the wait be brief"? O cursed

reminiscenze! Mi ostino a conficcare
nel tempo ciò che non è temporale.
Ho incontrato il divino in forme e modi
che ho sottratto al demonico senza sentirmi ladro.
Se una partita è in giuoco io non ne sono l'arbitro
e neppure l'urlante spettatore.
Me ne giunge notizia ma di rado.
Il mio tutore m'ha lasciato in margine
per una sua finezza particolare.
In tempo di carestia sono preziosi gli avanzi.
Non mi lusingo di essere prelibato,
non penso che l'infinito sia una mangiatoia
ma penso col mio mezzo limitato: il pensiero.
Non si pensa con l'occhio, non si guarda
con la testa. Parrebbe che i nostri sensi
siano male distribuiti. Oppure
è un mio difetto particolare. Meglio
una vita indivisa suddivisa
che un totale impensabile mostruoso;
o forse . . .

GLORIA DELLE VITE INUTILI

Siamo così legati al nostro corpo
da non immaginarne la sopravvivenza
che come un fiato, non un flatus vocis,
fatta eccezione per i soprassalti
di un tavolino che una versiera ad hoc
a modo suo manovri per far cassetta.
Ma una trasformazione che non sia
inidentità come può immaginarsi?
Così il grande e ventruto Kapdfer,
tale il nome di guerra benché non legato
a imprese eroiche o erotiche degne di un Margutte,
trent'anni fa un fantasma evanescente
distrutto dalla droga, poi risorto

memories! I stubbornly insist
on nailing what's not temporal onto time.
I've met the divine in forms and ways
I've borrowed from the demonic without feeling like a thief.
If there's a game being played I'm not the referee
nor the shouting spectator.
I hear news of it, but rarely.
My coach left me on the sidelines
thanks to a peculiar delicacy of his.
In times of want the remains are precious.
I don't fool myself that I was preferred,
I don't think the infinite is a trough
but I think with my limited means: with thought.
We don't think with the eye, don't look
with the brain. It seems our senses
are badly distributed. Or else
it's a peculiar defect of mine. Better
an undivided subdivided life
than an unthinkable monstrous whole;
or maybe . . .

THE GLORY OF USELESS LIVES

We are so bound to our bodies
we can only imagine survival
as a breath, not a flatus vocis,
except for the sudden starts of the table
that an ad hoc she-devil
maneuvers as she can to make a dime.
But a transformation that isn't non-identity—
how can it be imagined?
Thus the great and paunchy Kapdfer
(such was his nom de guerre though he wasn't involved
in heroic or erotic enterprises worthy of a Margutte),
thirty years ago an evanescent ghost
destroyed by drugs, then resurrected

tutto d'un pezzo non più riconoscibile
per la sublime sua inutilità,
compì il suo capo d'opera morendo
senza lasciare traccia che lo perpetui a lungo.
Chissà che
simili vite siano le sole autentiche,
ma perché, ma per chi? Si batte il capo
contro la biologia come se questa
avesse un senso o un'intenzione; ma
è troppo chiedere.

UNA MALATTIA

Se si rallenta la produzione
chissà dove andremo a finire
io non ho prodotto mai nulla
e so benissimo dove . . .

Anche gli omicidî entrano
nel fatturato del prodotto
mai io ho ucciso solo due tordi
e un passero solitario
mezzo secolo fa
e se anche il giudice chiuderà un occhio
non potrò fare altrettanto
affetto come sono dall'incurabile
imperdonabile malattia
della pietà.

Non ho molta fiducia d'incontrarti
nella vita eterna.
Era già problematico parlarti
nella terrena.

all in one piece, no longer recognizable
thanks to his sublime uselessness,
completed his masterpiece by dying
without leaving a trace to immortalize him for long.
Who knows
whether lives like his are the only authentic ones,
but why, but for whom? We butt our heads
against biology as if
it had a meaning or an intent; but
that's asking too much.

A MALADY

If we slow down production
who knows where we'll end up
I've never produced a thing
and I know very well where . . .

Murderers also play a role
in invoicing the product
But I've killed only two robins
and a "solitary sparrow"
half a century ago
and even if the judge turns a blind eye
I cannot do the same
afflicted as I am with the incurable
unpardonable malady
of pity.

I don't have much faith in meeting you
in eternity.
It was hard enough talking to you
on earth.

La colpa è nel sistema
delle comunicazioni.
Se ne scoprono molte ma non quella
che farebbe ridicole nonché inutili
le altre.

LA VITA IN PROSA

Il fatto è che la vita non si spiega
né con la biologia
né con la teologia.
La vita è molto lunga
anche quando è corta
come quella della farfalla –
la vita è sempre prodiga
anche quando la terra non produce nulla.
Furibonda è la lotta che si fa
per renderla inutile e impossibile.
Non resta che il pescaggio nell'inconscio
l'ultima farsa del nostro moribondo teatro.
Manderei ai lavori forzati o alla forca
chi la professa o la subisce. È chiaro che l'ignaro
è più che sufficiente per abbuiare il buio.

PER ALBUM

Assicurato
che il cuore non invecchia
il pentalaureato
si guarda nello specchio
con orrore.

The trouble lies in the system
of communications.
Many have been discovered but not the one
that would make the others ridiculous
as well as useless.

LA VIE EN PROSE

The fact is life is not explained
by biology
or theology.
Life is very long
even when it's short
like the butterfly's—
life is always prodigal
even when the earth produces nothing.
Furious the struggle we put up
to make it useless and impossible.
All that's left is fishing in the unconscious,
the last farce of our dying theater.
I'd sentence those who practice it, or submit,
to hard labor or the gallows. It's clear the ignorant
are more than sufficient to darken the darkness.

FOR AN ALBUM

Assured
that the heart never ages
the man weighed down with honors
looks into the mirror
with horror.

L'evoluzione biologica
ha un passo così lento che a quel metro
la lumaca è un fulmine.
C'è voluta non so che iradiddio
prima che fosse nato l'archetipo di un bipede.
Non è questo lo strano; lo strano è
che tutto ciò sembri lungimiranza.
Bisognerà trovare un altro nome
per spiegare l'arcano.

L'HAPAX

È scomparso l'hapax
l'unico esemplare di qualcosa
che si suppone esistesse al mondo.
Si evita di parlarne, qualcuno minimizza
l'evento, l'inevento. Altri sono aux abois
ma la costernazione è prevalente.
Fosse stato un uccello, un cane o almeno un uomo
allo stato selvatico. Ma si sa
solo che non c'è più e non può rifarsi.

Non so se Dio si sia reso conto
della grande macchina da lui costruita
un errore di calcolo dev'essere alla base
dell'universo; tanto è lungo il suo
edificarsi e rapido il suo crollo.
C'era qualcosa dapprincipio, poi
venne il tutto, vacuo e imprevedibile.

Biological evolution
proceeds so slowly that at its pace
the snail is lightning.
I don't know what cataclysm it took
before the archetype of a biped was born.
That's not what's strange; what's strange
is that it all looks like farsightedness.
We'll have to find another name
to explain the arcane.

THE HAPAX

The hapax has vanished
the one example of something
supposed to have existed in the world.
We avoid discussing it, some minimize
the event, the nonevent. Others are in despair
but dismay is prevalent.
It could have been a bird, a dog, or at least
a man in the savage state. But all we know
is that it is no more and can't come back.

I don't know if God has noticed
that in the great machine he built
an error in calculation must lie at the base
of the universe; so long in the construction,
so rapid its demise.
There was something at the outset,
then came the all, empty and unpredictable.

NON OCCORRONO TEMPI LUNGHI

per i cercatori di funghi
ma basta un battibaleno
per apprendere che non ha senso
buccinare di tempi vuoti o pieni.
Non esistono tempi corti
per fare che lo spazio si raggrumi
nel solo punto che conta
e sembra anche ridicolo parlare
di vivi e morti.

IT DOESN'T TAKE A LONG TIME

for the mushroom hunters
but an instant's enough
to learn there's no sense
trumpeting about time being empty or full.
There's no short time
in which space can come to a head
in the one point that counts
and it also seems ridiculous to speak
of living and dead.

TRANSLATOR'S ACKNOWLEDGMENTS

I am grateful to the Ingram Merrill Foundation and to my colleagues at Random House for making it possible for me to spend the summer of 1983 working on this translation in Italy. I would also like to thank William Arrowsmith, Irma Brandeis, Antonella Francini, and my editor, Erroll McDonald, for their close readings of the manuscript, which have contributed greatly to whatever merit these versions may have. Others who deserve a special word of appreciation include Virginia Avery, Frank Bidart, Harry Brewster, Harold Brodkey, Roberto Calasso, Maria Campbell, Annalisa Cima, Giovanna dalla Chiesa, James Fox, Arthur Goldwag, Daniel Halpern, Derek Johns, Jo Metsch, Howard Moss, Clotilde Peploe, Luciano Rebay, Niccolo Tucci, Helen Vendler, Rosanna Warren, William Weaver, Charles Wright, and, last but first, my wife, Susan Grace, my constant companion at the library table where most of this work was done.

NOTES

The dating of the poems and some of the other information presented in these notes is drawn from the Mondadori edition of *Altri versi*, edited by Giorgio Zampa, and from the Contini-Bettarini variorum edition of Montale's collected work, *L'opera in versi*. Though the headings give the titles of the translations, the notes occasionally deal with words or references in the Italian text.

Bibliographical information concerning Montale's writings may be found in the list of Further Readings, which follows the notes.

OTHERWISE

I

"Montale, Clizia e l'America," *Forum Italicum* 16, 3 (Winter 1982), pp. 171–202.

15   "Today." 1978. *Ratto d'Europa*: an untranslatable pun. The word *ratto* means both "rape" and "rat."

15   "Waiting." May 7, 1978.

17   "Our Upbringing." 1972. The operetta character Fanfan-la-Tulipe is also mentioned in the poem "Keepsake" in *Le occasioni*.

17   "Hypothesis II." The word *sfascio* (undoing) implies a reference to the *fascio* or bundle of sticks, the symbol of Italian Fascism.

19   "How the horizon . . ." September 4, 1976.

19   "The crust of the Earth is thinner . . ." August 26, 1979.

21   "The Allegory." 1978.

23   "With what joy . . ." 1976/1979. *Charabia* (French): unintelligible language, jargon, perhaps from the Arabic *algharbiya*, meaning "Western, or Berber, language."

23   "He's not cruel like Valéry's sparrow . . ." 1978. See "L'oiseau cruel" in Valéry's *Pièces diverses de toute époque*.

25   "The future already happened a while ago . . ." 1978.

25   "The big initial bang . . ." Probably 1979.

25   "It's probable I can say I . . ." Probably 1979.

27   "Time and Times II." 1979.

27   "The Oboe." 1979.

29   "The Performance." 1979.

29   "Had he who staged the cabaret . . ." Probably 1980.

30   "If the universe was born . . ." Probably 1980.

31   "You can be right . . ." Probably 1980. *Buridda*: a Genoese fish stew.

31   "Joviana." January 2, 1980.

33   "When my name appeared in almost all the papers . . ." January 14, 1980.

33   "In the East." January 8, 1980.

33   "At Dawn." Probably 1980.

35   "Monologue." Probably 1980. *Barnabites*: Pauline order of monks dedicated to education and missionary work. Montale studied with the Barnabite fathers in Genoa as a child. The coach is mentioned in the story "Laguzzi e C." in *Farfalla di Dinard*.

37   "Pupil of the Muses." 1980.

II

39   "To My Friend Pea." February 4, 1978. Enrico Pea (1881–1958), Versilian novelist, poet, and playwright, is best known for his *Moscardino* trilogy of novels. *Leopoldo Fregoli* (1867–1936) was a renowned variety actor and quick-change artist.

41   "Nixon in Rome." March 2, 1969.

43   "Càffaro." 1972. *Il Càffaro* was a Genoese liberal-democratic newspaper (1875–1929) founded by A. G. Barrili and named after the medieval Genoese politician and annalist (1080–1164). Flavio *Andò* (1851–1915), a Sicilian, was the best-known interpreter of turn-of-the-century Italian romantic comedy, playing as leading man opposite Eleonora Duse for seven years.

43   "At the Giardino d'Italia." 1978. Valery *Larbaud* (1881–1957), French poet, critic and translator, best known for his *Poems of A. O. Barna-*

booth, was the leading French enthusiast of Italian letters in the early twentieth century. He was instrumental in establishing Italo Svevo's international reputation; Montale, in turn, wrote several articles which led to a reevaluation of Svevo's work in Italy. *Bigarrée*: disparate, various.

45   "This was thirty, maybe forty, years ago . . ." 1979. *Charles Singleton* is an esteemed American scholar and translator of Dante. See also the poem "Clizia Says."

45   "Succulents." September 3, 1978. Cesare *de Lollis* (1863–1928) was a humanist critic, editor of *La cultura*, professor at Genoa and Rome.

47   "Booby." September 5, 1978. *Palmaria*: an island off Portovenere on the Ligurian coast near the Cinque Terre, or Five Towns, where Montale spent the summers in his youth. There is a naval fortress on the island.

49   "A Visitor." 1979.

49   "The Hiding Places II." 1978. *The solitary sparrow*: a reference to Leopardi's poem "Il passero solitario." J. H. Whitfield notes in his edition of Leopardi's *Canti* (Manchester University Press, 1967) that "this bird has a long literary pedigree," starting with Psalm 102:7, "I watch, and am as a sparrow alone upon the house top," which was imitated by Petrarch and then adopted by Leopardi. According to Whitfield, however, the *passero solitario* is not a sparrow at all but "blue rock thrush, a local variety of thrush." *Manon*: Massenet's 1884 opera, like Puccini's later *Manon Lescaut*, is based on the Abbé Prévost's novel of 1731, *L'Histoire du chevalier des Grieux et de Manon Lescaut*. *Corniglia*: one of the towns of the Cinque Terre.

51   "Bloody October." 1979. *Mesco*: cape on the Ligurian Riviera between Levanto and Monterosso, the town in the Cinque Terre where the Montale villa was situated. See "Punta del Mesco" in *Le occasioni*.

53   "An Invitation to Lunch." 1978. The occasion for the poem is also described in the article "Da Gerusalemme divisa" published in the *Corriere della Sera* on January 6, 1964, and included in Montale's book of travel writings, *Fuori di casa*.

55   "Doubt." 1979.

55   "(Something Like) Glory." November 10, 1978. Afrikan Aleksandrovich *Spir* (Ukraine, 1837–Geneva, 1890) was a religious spiritualist philosopher who wrote in German and French.

57   "It seems impossible . . ." Probably 1979.

57   "No more news . . ." Probably 1979. Montale's wife, Drusilla Tanzi, who died in 1963, is buried in the graveyard of the church of San Felice a Ema, just south of Florence. Montale is now buried there as well.

59   " Wipe your misty glasses . . ." Probably 1979.

59   "My Swiss watch had the tic . . ." Probably 1979. The scene is also described in the first section of "Due prose veneziane" in *Satura*.

61   "Luni, etc." Luni was a prosperous ancient Etruscan city at the eastern end of Liguria, near the present-day town of Sarzana. Its port, the Roman *Portus Lunae*, was located on the Gulf of La Spezia. Luni was much diminished by malaria in the Roman era and was sacked by the Vandals in the fifth century. Petrarch mentions it as an example of the transience of human things, and Dante refers to it in *Par.* XVI, 73–78. Earlier drafts indicate that this poem is addressed to Clizia.

61   "I have such faith in you . . ." Probably 1979. C. once again is Clizia. See note to "Brooding," above.

63   "Clizia Says." 1979. Author's note: "The scholar is Charles Singleton, whom I never forgot (as if it were possible!). The monsignor of the fleas is John Donne, who is fashionable today." See also "This was thirty, maybe forty years ago," and the poems "The Fleas" and "Prose for A. M.," above.

63   "Clizia in '34." January 5, 1980.

65   "Predictions." 1977.

65   "Inside/Outside." 1976. "*Annalena*": Pensione with a beautiful private garden in the Via Romana in Florence, near the Boboli Gardens.

67   "In '38." 1978.

69   "Foursome." 1979. Originally titled "Dopopalio," i.e., "After the Palio." For information on Montale's friend the Ligurian poet Camillo Sbarbaro (1888–1967), an important influence on Montale's early work, see "Recollections of Sbarbaro" and "Intentions: Imaginary Interview" in Galassi, trans., *The Second Life of Art*. Elena Vivante "was the daughter of a very notable poet who is no longer read: Adolfo De Bosis. She married a philosopher who was enamored of English poetry, Leone Vivante, who like her was unsuited to business or practical life. The couple started a family and lived at Solaia, a villa in the countryside not far from Siena, surrounded by a throng of itinerant and burdensome friends" (*Sulla poesia*, p. 327).

69   "Since Life is Fleeing . . ." January 20, 1980.

71   "Credo." 1978. The Italian text erroneously states that Bard College is in New Jersey, not New York.

73   "To Claudia Muzio." February 10, 1978. Muzio (1892–1936) was the leading Italian soprano of her era, and she sang both in Europe and America. Montale once called Maria Callas the most inspired operatic actress since Muzio (see *Prime alla Scala*, p. 325).

73   "When the Blackcap . . ." 1978.

75   "Beloved of the Gods." October 30, 1978. *Un barba*: Piedmontese expression (*barba* = beard) for a Protestant or, by extension, an old man.

75   "A Visit." June 13, 1978.

77   "Note on 'A Visit.'" 1978.

79   "Ah!" 1976. On the typescript of this poem Montale wrote: "Perhaps the book could end with this poem."

UNCOLLECTED POEMS

EARLY POEMS, 1918–1928

83   "Elegy." First published in Silvio Ramat, ed., *Omaggio a Montale* (Milano: Mondadori, 1966), with the date January 26, 1918.

85   "Montale at War." This poem was written on a postcard sent from the war zone in the Trentino on October 7, 1918, to the critic and poet Sergio Solmi, whom Montale had befriended in 1917 during an officers' training course at the Palazzo della Pilotta in Parma. Solmi quoted it from memory—with a few slight variations—in his article "Parma 1917" in *La fiera letteraria* VIII, 28 (July 12, 1953), now reprinted in Montale's *Quaderno genovese*, ed. Laura Barile. Solmi says in part: "In the last two lines of this occasional quatrain it seems to me that there is already all of Montale (behind it, clearly, are Sbarbaro, Govoni, the Ligurian and Lacerbian experiments, but the new note is unmistakable)."

For a discussion of the poem see Lanfranco Caretti, "Ancora per l'Ur-Montale," *Paragone* 346 (December 1978), pp. 27–29.

85   "Silent Music." A manuscript of this poem dated "Monte Loner, October 1918" is among Montale's papers at the University of Pavia. It was published, with notes by Maria Antonietta Grignani, in *Strumenti critici* VII, 21–22 (October 1973), pp. 220–24. Grignani calls it "a poem strongly suggested by a musical idea"; in this respect it is close to the "Accordi," written at about the same time, and to the poem "Musica sognata" of 1923, published in the first edition of *Ossi di seppia* but later excluded. These attempts at imitating music show the young Montale trying in part, as Grignani puts it, "to avoid the prosaic-ironic mode of crepuscularism," the dominant poetic school of the early twentieth century, which, largely in reaction to the florid rhetoric of D'Annunzio, wrote about disillusion, nostalgia, and simple things in a straightforward manner. Among the leading *crepuscolari*, many of whom later became futurists, were Gozzano, Corazzini, Govoni, and Palazzeschi. For an illuminating discussion of the movement and its influence, see Joseph Cary's excellent *Three Modern Italian Poets: Saba, Ungaretti, Montale* (New York: New York University Press, 1969), especially chapter 1.

Giacomo Debenedetti, editor of the Turin journal *Primo Tempo*, which had published "Accordi" earlier that year, wrote to Montale on December 29, 1922, accepting "Riviere," "L'agave su lo scoglio," and "I limoni," but adding about "Accordi" that it showed "some affinities with the *crepuscolari*, though with more serene successes and more disenchanted reprises. . . . 'Musica silenziosa,' and 'A galla,' after the developments I have seen from you, bring me nothing new; extremely refined technical experiments, against a background of sensations whose name and position in the history of poetic motifs are well known."

89   "Floating." 1919. A revised version was published in the pamphlet *Satura* of 1962 (see notes to "Fan for Sandra F." below).

91   "Piano Sonatina." June 1919. The poem was first published in an article by Lanfranco Caretti, "Un inedito montaliano," *Paragone* XXIX, 336 (February 1978), pp. 3–7. Sergio Solmi, who owned the manuscript, wrote to Montale on January 21, 1923: "In the first ('Accordi,' 'Musica silenziosa,' etc.) a residue of decadent and crepuscular themes was evident (I still have, in a drawer, your 'Suonatina di Pianoforte' which confirms this impression) but which in you seems to me more literary (in the good sense) than otherwise. Which is what saves you. In an old letter of yours, if I recall correctly, you told me: free verse, discursivity, fine."

This ironic and parodistic poem, which almost seems to refute the two that precede it, owes much to Laforgue and Govoni, Caretti points out, and also to the nonsensical surrealism of Palazzeschi and the futurist free-verse poets. "It allows us to situate the Montale of these years on the innovative side of poetry-as-negation, typical above all of the dramatic crisis of the war: on the side, that is, which carries out once and for all the pitiless burying of both crepuscularism and D'Annunzianism."

93   "Chords." Written sometime between 1916 and 1920 (see below). Published in *Primo Tempo*, Turin, June 15, 1922, along with "Riviere," which was later included in *Ossi di seppia*, as was the sixth section of the group, "Corno inglese."

Montale wrote Giacinto Spagnoletti on August 27, 1960 (quoted in

Spagnoletti's article "Preistoria di Montale," in Silvio Ramat, ed., *Omaggio a Montale*, [Mondadori, 1966] pp. 121–22):

I could not give a date to ["Chords"] with absolute precision; they certainly postdate the first real and proper *osso* ("Meriggiare [pallido e assorto]" of 1916) but are much earlier than "Riviere" (March 1920), the poem that summed up my juvenilia, inserted by me in the *Ossi* even if it sits there uncomfortably (it is a synthesis written before the analysis!). The "Corno inglese" was the only one that could be lifted out of the series: whose general sense, along with the ingenuous pretense of imitating musical instruments (not to mention the bit of starch that can be found here and there) displeased me, and still does. I must therefore conclude that in my youthful *château d'eaux* (as Lorenzo Montano called my poetry) alongside a more troubled vein, or even *within* that vein, the thinner but more limpid vein of the *Ossi* was making its way for a long while. The entire opening section of the *Ossi* (except for "In limine," a poem strangely misunderstood by my anthologists) thus belongs to the pro-Montale: and in this group belong— though even within these limits I later rejected them—the poems of "Accordi."

See also Montale's discussion of his early work in "Intentions: Imaginary Interview" in Galassi, trans., *The Second Life of Art*.

101 "Here where many years ago by now . . ." Late 1922 or early 1923.

103 "Levantine Letter." February–June 1923.

109 "Let's go down the road that slopes . . ." August 1923.

111 "Ceccardo slept under this damp arch sometimes . . ." 1923. Ceccardo Roccatagliata Ceccardi (1871–1919) was a Ligurian poet and journalist best known for his *Il viandante* (The Wayfarer) of 1904. A decadent poet in classic form, who influenced both Sbarbaro and Montale, he adopted the itinerant traveler's *maudit* role in life and in art. Montale wrote of him in "Intentions: Imaginary Interview" that "he never really understood his instrument. He lived facing the past, always in need of academic recognition. Far from proclaiming himself a boy wonder, he was too suspicious of the child within. Still, none of his contemporaries had a voice comparable to his in stretches."

Lunigiana: region around La Spezia on the Tuscan coast, once controlled by the ancient Etruscan city of Luni (see notes to "Luni, etc." above).

111 "Gulls." October 1923.

113 "In the Void." Published in the 1962 privately printed *Satura*, with the date 1924.

115 "Good Linuccia, climbing up . . ." Fragment of 1926 addressed to Linuccia Saba, daughter of Montale's friend the Triestine poet Umberto Saba. Discussed in Lanfranco Caretti, "Testi montaliani inediti," *Il Ponte* XXXIII, 4–5 (30 April–31 August 1977), pp. 487–94.

Montale apparently made a brief trip to Trieste in May 1926 to visit Svevo and Saba. Montale wrote to Caretti, "In 1926 Linuccia was a graceful girl. It may be she never even saw this piece."

For Caretti, the fragment is significant evidence of Montale's transition from the style of *Ossi di seppia* to the more closed objective-correlative method of *Le occasioni*. He notes the Dantesque invocation of Linuccia as the poet's female companion in confronting the "hell" of the contemporary world and sees her as a kind of precursor of the *donna salutifera* who appears in *Le occasioni*. The fragment also bears comparison with an unfinished translation of Eliot's "Ash Wednesday." The year 1926, it should be noted, marked the beginning of the Fascist hegemony in Italy. This was also the year when Montale's first publisher and early champion, the liberal Piero Gobetti, went into exile in France.

115 "Sweet years whose long refractions . . ." 1926. At one time or another this poem has been called "Prima della primavera ("Before Spring") and "Destino di Arletta" ("Arletta's Destiny"). See a discussion of the poem by Maria Antonietta Grignani, *Strumenti critici* VII, 21–22, (October 1973), pp. 221–23.

Grignani calls this an important text "for the internal history of Montale's poetry," noting the appearance of the inspirational female figure in the later part of the poem.

117 "You say our destinies of yesteryear have been recast . . ." Probably 1928. This fragment, the only known instance of a poem by Montale written in French, is a precursor of the 1928 "Carnevale di Gerti," one of the best-known poems in *Le occasioni*. Montale wrote to the poet Angelo Barile on July 6, 1932, about the "Carnevale": "Gerti was and is a lady from Graz. She had a soldier for a husband . . . and saw him only when he was on leave. On New Year's Day we had drawn lots for some gifts for friends in Trieste and for them also played a sorcerer's trick that is fairly often used in the north. Throw a spoonful of melted lead per person into a cup of cold water and from the strange solidified deformations that result deduce the destiny of each."

LATER POEMS, 1962–1977

119 "Fan for Sandra F." 1962. First published in a privately printed pamphlet entitled *Satura*, issued for the marriage of Alessandra (Sandra) Fagiuoli and Gabriele Crespi on December 22, 1962, by the Officina Bodoni, Verona. The booklet also includes: "A galla," "Minstrels" (published in the first edition of *Ossi di seppia* as "Musica sognata"), "Nel vuoto," and "Botta e risposta" (later published in *Satura*, 1971). The genesis of "Fan for Sandra F." is discussed in Vittore Branca, "Ultimi scartafacci di *Satura*," in Silvio Ramat, ed., *Omaggio a Montale*, pp. 393–97.

119 "Bobi's Mother." March 17, 1968. For a portrait of Montale's friend B.B., see "In Memory of Roberto Bazlen" in *The Second Life of Art*.

121 "Refrain of the Honorable Professor." August 10, 1968.

121 "La Belle Dame Sans Merci II." 26 October–10 November 1968.

123 "Second Footnote." October 28, 1968.

123 "The 3." November 3, 1968.

125 "Precautions." November 15, 1968.

125 "Little Diary." December 2, 1968.

127 "Near Lodi." February 26, 1969. *Quagliodromo*: rifle range where hunters practice shooting quail.

127 "The Drama." February 26, 1969.

129 "Moving." March 19–20, 1969.

129 "Reading the Paper." April 6, 1969.

129 "Poetry throughout . . ." April 7, 1969.

131 "For longer than a century . . ." April 20, 1969.

FURTHER READING

Writings of Eugenio Montale

POETRY

Ossi di seppia [Cuttlefish Bones]. Torino: Gobetti, 1925. New editions in 1928, 1931, 1939, 1942; first Mondadori edition, 1948.

Le occasioni [The Occasions]. Torino: Einaudi, 1939. New edition, 1940; first Mondadori edition, 1949. Contains the poems originally published in *La casa dei doganieri e altri versi* [The Customs House and Other Poems] (Firenze: Vallechi, 1939).

Quaderno di traduzioni [Notebook of Translations]. Milano: Edizioni della Meridiana, 1948. First Mondadori edition, 1975.

La bufera e altro [The Tempest and Other Things]. Venezia: Neri Pozza, 1956. First Mondadori edition, 1957. Includes the poems published in *Finisterre* (Lugano: Collana di Lugano, 1943).

Satura [Miscellany]. Milano: Arnoldo Mondadori Editore, 1971. Not to be confused with the privately published pamphlet issued under the same title in 1962.

Diario del '71 e del '72 [Diary of 1971 and 1972]. Milano: Arnoldo Mondadori Editore, 1973.

Quaderno di quattro anni [Notebook of Four Years]. Milano: Arnoldo Mondadori Editore, 1977.

Tutte le poesie [Collected Poems]. Milano: Arnoldo Mondadori Editore, 1977.

L'opera in versi [Poetical Works]. Bibliographically annotated variorum edition of the collected poems, ed. Gianfranco Contini and Rosanna Bettarini. Torino: Einaudi, 1980.

Altri versi e poesie disperse [Other and Uncollected Poems], ed. Giorgio Zampa. Milano: Arnoldo Mondadori Editore, 1981. Contains the previously uncollected work first published in *L'opera in versi*, with some additions.

PROSE

Farfalla di Dinard [Butterfly at Dinard]. Venezia: Neri Pozza, 1956. First Mondadori edition, 1960; new edition 1969. Autobiographical/fictional sketches.

Eugenio Montale / Italo Svevo: Lettere, con gli scritti di Montale su Svevo [The Montale–Svevo Letters, with Montale's writings on Svevo]. Bari: De Donato, 1966. Published by Mondadori as *Italo Svevo-Eugenio Montale: Carteggio* [Correspondence], ed. Giorgio Zampa, 1976.

Auto da Fé: Cronache in due tempi [Act of Faith: Chronicles from Two Periods]. Milano: Il Saggiatore, 1966. Cultural criticism drawn mainly from the pages of the *Corriere della Sera* (ed. Giorgio Zampa).

Fuori di casa [Away from Home]. Milano-Napoli: Ricciardi, 1969. First Mondadori edition, 1975. Travel writing and reportage.

La poesia non esiste [Poetry Doesn't Exist]. Milano: Scheiwiller, 1971. Cultural burlesques.

Nel nostro tempo [In Our Time], ed. Riccardo Campa. Milano: Rizzoli, 1972. Anthology of extracts from Montale's cultural criticism.

Sulla poesia [On Poetry], ed. Giorgio Zampa. Milano: Arnoldo Mondadori Editore, 1976. Collected critical writings on poetry and poets.

Lettere a Quasimodo [Letters to Quasimodo], ed. Sebastiano Grasso. Milano: Bompiani, 1981. Chronicles Montale's relationship with the poet Quasimodo in the thirties, giving a vivid picture of literary life in Florence in this period.

Prime alla Scala [Openings at La Scala], ed. Gianfranca Lavezzi. Milano: Arnoldo Mondadori Editore, 1981. Collected writings on music.

Quaderno genovese [Genoa Notebook], ed. Laura Barile. Milano: Arnoldo Mondadori Editore, 1983. Annotated edition of a notebook kept by Montale in 1917; an important index of the sources and formation of his ideas.

Notable English Translations of Montale

Sergio Pacifici, ed. and trans., *The Promised Land and Other Poems: An Anthology of Four Contemporary Italian Poets*. New York: S. F. Vanni, 1957.

Edwin Morgan, trans., *Poems from Eugenio Montale*. Reading, England: School of Art, University of Reading, 1959.

Robert Lowell, *Imitations*. New York: Farrar, Straus & Cudahy, 1961.

Quarterly Review of Literature XI, 4 (Spring 1962). Montale issue, ed. Irma Brandeis. Annandale-on-Hudson, New York: Bard College.

Carlo Golino, ed. and trans., *Contemporary Italian Poetry: An Anthology*. Berkeley and Los Angeles: University of California Press, 1962.

George Kay, trans., *Eugenio Montale: Poems*. Edinburgh: University Press. 1964.

Glauco Cambon, ed., *Eugenio Montale: Selected Poems*. New York: New Directions, 1965. Various translators. Includes poems from *Ossi di seppia*, *Le occasioni*, and *La bufera e altro*.

Robin Fulton, trans., *An Italian Quartet: Saba, Ungaretti, Montale, Quasimodo*. London: London Magazine Editions, 1966.

George Kay, trans., *Selected Poems of Eugenio Montale*. London: Penguin Books, 1969.

G. Singh, trans., *The Butterfly of Dinard*. London: London Magazine Editions, 1970.

Edith Farnsworth, trans., *Provisional Conclusions: A Selection of the Poetry of Eugenio Montale*. Chicago: Henry Regnery Company, 1970. Translations of most of the poems from Montale's first three books not included in the New Directions *Selected Poems*.

G. Singh, trans., *Xenia*. Los Angeles: Black Sparrow Press and New Directions, 1970.

Agenda Vol. 9, No. 4–Vol. 10, No. 1 (Autumn–Winter 1971–72), Yeats/Montale issue, ed. William Cookson. Contains translations of 27 poems by Keith Bosley, G. Singh, and Bernard Wall, as well as several brief essays.

Lawrence Kart, trans., *The Motets of Eugenio Montale*. San Francisco: Grabhorn-Hoyem Press, 1974.

Cid Corman, trans., poems in *The Gist of Origin: 1951–1971: An Anthology*, ed. Cid Corman. New York: Grossman Publishers, 1975.

Jonathan Galassi, trans., *Xenia*, in *Ploughshares* 2, 4 (1975). Cambridge, Mass. Reprinted in *The Pushcart Prize: Best of the Small Presses*, edited by Bill Henderson (Yonkers, New York: Pushcart Book Press, 1976).

G. Singh, trans., *New Poems: A Selection from* Satura *and* Diario del '71 e del '72. New York: New Directions, 1976. Contains F. R. Leavis's essay on *Xenia*.

Alastair Hamilton, trans., *Poet in Our Time*. New York: Urizen Books, 1976. Translation of *Nel nostro tempo*.

Kate Hughes, trans., *Xenia and Motets*. London: Agenda Editions [1977].

Pequod II, 2 (Winter 1977): *Eugenio Montale: Poetry and Prose*, ed. Jonathan Galassi.

Charles Wright, trans., *The Storm and Other Poems*. Field Translation Series 1. Oberlin, Ohio: Oberlin College, 1977.

G. Singh, trans., *Selected Essays*. Manchester, England: Carcanet New Press Ltd., 1978.

G. Singh, trans., *It Depends: A Poet's Notebook*. New York: New Directions, 1980. Translation of *Quaderno di quattro anni*.

Charles Wright, trans., *Mottetti/Motets*. Ames, Iowa: The Windhover Press at the University of Iowa, 1981.

Jonathan Galassi, trans., *The Second Life of Art: Selected Essays of Eugenio Montale*. New York: The Ecco Press, 1982.

William Arrowsmith, trans., *Eugenio Montale: The Storm*. New York: Horizon Press, forthcoming.

EUGENIO MONTALE was born in Genoa on Columbus Day, 1896. The publication of his first book, *Ossi di seppia*, in 1925, established him as the leading poet of his generation and an inspiration for intellectuals opposed to Fascism. *Le occasioni* (1939) and *La bufera e altro* (1956) confirmed his stature as the greatest Italian poet since Leopardi.

After World War II, Montale moved from Florence, where he had lived since the late twenties, to Milan, where he became chief literary critic—and later musical critic as well—for Italy's principal newspaper, the *Corriere della Sera*. *Satura*, published in 1971, marked his return to poetry after a long hiatus, in a radically new, more informal and epigrammatic style. Three more collections of poems were to follow: *Diario del '71 e del '72* (1973), *Quaderno di quattro anni* (1977) and *Altri versi* (1981).

In addition to his distinguished work as a journalist, Montale also published numerous essays, stories and translations, and was a talented amateur painter. He was made a member for life of the Italian Senate in 1967, and in 1975 was awarded the Nobel Prize for Literature. He died in Milan on September 12, 1981.

JONATHAN GALASSI is an editor at Random House in New York and is also poetry editor of the *Paris Review*. His edition of Montale's selected essays, *The Second Life of Art*, was published in 1981. He received a grant from the Ingram Merrill Foundation for his work on this translation.